Democracy, Education, and Governance

SUNY Series, Global Conflict and Peace Education

Betty A. Reardon, Editor

Democracy, Education, and Governance

A Developmental Conception

Dale T. Snauwaert

State University of New York Press

Published by
State University of New York Press, Albany

© 1993 State University of New York

For information, address State University of New York Press,
State University Plaza, Albany, N.Y. 12246

Production by M. R. Mulholland
Marketing by Theresa A. Swierzowski

Library of Congress Cataloging-in-Publication Data
Snauwaert, Dale T., 1955–
    Democracy, education, and governance : a developmental conception
/ by Dale T. Snauwaert.
        p. cm. — (SUNY series, global conflict and peace education)
    Includes bibliographical references (p.) and index.
    ISBN 0-7914-1459-0 (alk. paper). — ISBN 0-7914-1460-4 (pbk. :
alk. paper)
    1. School management and organization—United States. 2. Teacher
participation in administration—United States.
3. Schools—Decentralization—United States. 4. School management and
organization—Illinois—Chicago—Case Studies. 5. School management
and organization—Kentucky—Case studies. I. Title. II. Series.
LB2805.S682   1993
371.2'00973—dc20   92-19819
                                                                      CIP

10 9 8 7 6 5 4 3 2 1

For my parents
Larry and Millie

Contents

Foreword

Dale Snauwaert's consideration of fundamental issues of school governance is presented within this series on peace and global issues because it offers a framework for understanding most conflicts in public policy from global security issues to decisions on hospital services in inner cities. It gives us not only a way of looking at questions related to educational purposes and decision making, but provides, as well, a mode of understanding some of the processes at work in the disintegration and reconstitution of nation states and urban communities. The crises we face at all levels emerge in large part from competing concepts of democracy, and the growing alienation between citizens and governments. That the 1992 Los Angeles riots and other such "civil disturbances" occurred simultaneously with the political cataclysms in Eastern Europe, and the dissipation of armed struggles in the Americas where the leadership of both sides has lost the trust of those who had once rallied to their ideological banners is indicative of this growing division between government and the people. The question of the "New World Order" is not, "What will it take to push forward the trend toward democracy in the world?" but rather "What form of democracy is emerging, who will participate in its design; and how will it effect the quality of life for the majority of the human family?" Similar queries are woven through Snauwaert's reflections and arguments for democratic school governance.

The current demand for self determination of persons who identify themselves by sexual orientation, religious belief, ethnic group, political party or nation is part of the world wide struggle for broadened participation in social policy formation and decision making. It is an assertion of the human capacity to create our own social realities. The development of that capacity is a primary purpose of peace education. Thus, Snauwaert's arguments for developmental democracy are a complement to the arguments of peace education that humans have innate capacities for social construction as well as personal development; that the processes of social and personal evolution are interrelated, probably interdependent. These arguments are imbedded in a notion of peace as the presence of community, a notion that echoes the concepts of the good society articulated by the five philosophers Snauwaert cites in making his case for the developmental conception of democracy. What he argues for is essentially a peacemaking approach to school governance that might well be applied to international institutions and global governance.

His arguments echo what peace educators have claimed for many years—that effective peace education can not take place within schools as they are currently structured and governed. The efficiency values that have lead to the notion of "product" and "growth" as primary educational goals are not conducive to community building or to true equality or authentic participation, the hallmarks of a society at peace. Educators the world over are calling for a reassessment of the values that guide educational policy and practice, and UNESCO proposes to reintroduce humanistic values into education. Such reintroduction is impossible under the essentially elitist form of governance that controls our schools. School governance is a crucial issue in peace education. It is my hope that many peace educators will read this volume.

Snauwaert demonstrates the possibility of a governance system which is simultaneously participative *and* sensitive to collective concerns. It is a system premised on shared sovereignty. Most serious students of world order hold that only through some similar system can a viable and just world peace be achieved and maintained.

Dale Snauwaert has given us cause for hope and a working plan for actualizing it. He has outlined the conditions of school governance in which education for peace can be most effectively pursued. He has opened for discussion a fundamental issue of education that lies at the heart of learning to construct a democratic education for global community.

Betty A. Reardon, Teachers College
Series Editor, Columbia University
July 1992

Preface

This book has its origins in my dual interests in democracy as a system of human relations and the process of human development. I discovered during the course of my graduate education that the developmental conception of democracy offered an integration of these two interests. I was taken by the power of this idea and decided, upon discovering that Chicago teachers took a similar position in their fight against bureaucracy in the Progressive Era, to attempt a thought experiment that asks, If our primary value is human development, how would we design our systems of school governance?

A number of people have been instrumental in the process that gave rise to this book and its publication. First, I would like to thank Jim Clarke, Fred Coombs, Ralph Page, Steve Tozer, and Phil Zodhiates for their constructive criticism. The anonymous reviewers of this manuscript also provided helpful comments. I would especially like to thank Betty Reardon for her insight, encouragement, and support. Finally, my wife, Mary, provided unending encouragement and significant insight.

Introduction

This book constitutes a study of and a exercise in "constitutional choice." In the *Declaration of Independence*, Thomas Jefferson asserts that "whenever any form of government becomes destructive of these ends [life, liberty, and happiness], it is the Right of the People to alter or to abolish it, and to institute new Government, laying its foundation on such principles and organizing its power in such form as to them shall seem most likely to effect their Safety and Happiness" (cited in Becker 1958, 8). In keeping with this right, *The Federalist Papers* begins with Hamilton questioning "whether societies of men are really capable or not of establishing good government from reflection and choice, or whether they are forever destined to depend for their political constitutions on accident and force" (cited in Ostrom 1987, 15). The remainder of *The Federalist Papers* is an argument affirming the former. As Vincent Ostrom points out in his seminal work *The Political Theory of a Compound Republic* (1987), implicit in both of the quotations above is the political notion of "constitutional choice," the principle that "human beings can exercise choice in creating systems of government" (4).[1]

As implied in the Jefferson quotation, constitutional choice entails the articulation of political principles, consistent with cherished values, from which the design features of particular governmental structures are derived. For example, liberty was one of the most cherished values that Madison and Hamilton held. In order to guarantee this value, they invoked the principle of "political constraint," the proposition that, given the self-interested and fallible nature of human beings, those exercising governmental prerogatives need to be constrained (checked). As Hamilton put it, "the passions of men will not conform to the dictates of reason and justice [thereby endangering liberty] without constraint" (cited in Ostrom 1987, 47).

From this principle, the design specifications of separation of powers and a compound structure were derived. As Madison observed, "The accumulation of all powers. . . in the same hands, whether of one, or few or many, and whether hereditary, self-appointed, or elective, will lead to tyranny" (cited in Ostrom 1987, 85). Implicit in this idea is the proposition that political constraint, and hence liberty, is contingent upon the separation of powers both within and across governmental units. Power can most effectively be constrained through a compound rather than a unitary republic wherein autonomous and limited governments with overlapping jurisdictions coexist, and where governmental offices with separate powers within each level are divided in order to check and balance each other. These design specifications comprise the basic blueprint of American constitutional government.

Constitutional choice, in addition, is not limited to the initial formation of a government, but it applies equally to the modification of an already existing form, as was the case with the framing of the American Constitution, a modification of confederation. In addition, constitutional choice is not restricted to the establishment of national governments, but it also applies equally to "all institutions of human governance" (Ostrom 1987, 5).[2] The overarching purpose of this book is to apply constitutional choice to the modification of school governance.

A number of scholars (e.g., Elmore 1987; Goodlad 1984; Grant 1985; Sirotnik and Clark 1988; Walberg et al. 1989) have argued that the way authority is structured and exercised shapes the intellectual and moral character of the school, thereby profoundly influencing student development. The current administrative structure of schools is highly centralized and bureaucratic. Principals, teachers, and parents have little say in decisions concerning curriculum, budgets, hiring of staff, goals and objectives, and the selection of books and materials (Lomotey and Swanson 1989).[3] Given the demonstrated importance of leadership, teacher competence, and parental involvement (Benson and Malone 1987; Erlandson and Bifano 1987; Geisert 1988; Guthrie 1986; Walberg 1984), the centralized authority structures of schools may contribute to poor educational performance.

The current system of school governance has its origins in the administrative reforms of the Progressive Era. The essence of this reform movement was the destruction of the decentralized ward system and the centralization of authority in the hands of educational experts and small, citywide school boards comprised predominately of business and professional men.

These reforms were premised upon the value of efficiency. Due to a number of socioeconomic changes, especially severe deflationary spirals in the economy, urbanization, and widespread immigration, organizational and social efficiency became prominent in the minds of reformers. The concern for efficiency was so pervasive—and took on such an evangelistic tone—that the historian Sammual Haber described it as a "Secular Great Awakening" (1964, ix).

Corresponding to the value of efficiency was the political principle of control. Efficiency demanded expert control of markets, the production process, city government, and the educational system. It was thought that a decentralized decision making process based upon political compromise was inherently wasteful both in terms of the process itself and its product: politically rather than scientifically derived policy. To ensure that policy was based upon "scientific" knowledge, the decision-making process needed to be controlled by "experts," those versed in scientific method. Typifying this outlook was Charles Eliot, the President of Harvard University: "The democracy must learn, in governmental affairs, whether municipal, state or national, to employ experts and abide by their decisions" (1989, 196). Eliot maintained that the purpose of "democratic education" was to "train the minds of the children that when they become adults they should...have respect for the attainments of experts in every branch of governmental, industrial, and social activity" (1989, 196).

In turn, the organizational structures of institutions were designed in terms of the specifications of centralized authority and bureaucratic administration. The result was a highly centralized, bureaucratic system of school governance (see chapter 1), which limited popular representation, insulating policymakers from the demands of working and lower-middle-class interests, including teachers.

The argument for centralization was premised upon the proposition that it was an inevitable consequence of industrial development and urbanization. It is also apparent that these reformers sought a correspondence between the organization of industry and the organization of schooling. The school was modeled after the factory. Such correspondence was premised on the value of efficiency not as an abstract value, but conceived in terms of the efficient integration of students into a hierarchical labor force. This integration could best be achieved through a bureaucratic model of schooling entailing a system of input, behavior, and output controls mirroring the factory.

This book is premised, however, upon the historical position that the bureaucratic rationalization of industry and schooling, premised upon efficiency, was not the inevitable result of the logic of industrial development nor urban growth. Rather, it was an alternative "constitutionally chosen." Centralization was a strategy freely chosen to ensure greater control of the production process and the reproduction of an industrial labor force. However, viable alternatives formed the basis of resistance in both industry and schooling. For example, the Chicago Teachers' Federation (CTF), lead by Margaret

Haley and supported by Ella Flagg Young, waged a twenty-year campaign in opposition to bureaucratic rationalization.[4] Haley argued that the centralization of decision-making authority would make "the teacher an automaton, a mere factory hand, whose duty is to carry out mechannically and unquestionably the ideas and order of those clothed with the authority of position" (1903b, 2). Young maintained that centralization would turn teachers "into a class of assistants, whose duty consists in carrying out instructions of a higher class which originates method for all" (1901, 107). Young also argued that if every aspect of educational policy were dictated by a central authority, then the very essence "of that form of activity known as the teacher" would be undermined (1901, 39).

Implicit in these and other such responses to the centralization of educational authority (see chapter 1) is the value of professional and, more broadly, human development. Haley and Young opposed centralization on the basis that disallowing teachers from participation in the policymaking process would undermine their development as teachers, as well as undermine the educational process itself. These educators recognized a conflict between the efficiency demands of capitalist, industrial development, embodied in the reproductive function of schooling, and the developmental function of schooling (broadly conceived as affecting both educators and students). A similar position is taken by such correspondence theorists as Bowles and Gintis (1976). However, although highly critical of bureaucratic rationalization, correspondence theory also assumes its inevitability within a capitalist society (Apple 1982). My position, following Apple (1982) among others (e.g., Hogan 1985), is that this inevitability is historically inaccurate, that alternatives, including a developmental alternative, were viable.

In addition, implicit in these two alternatives (bureaucracy and decentralization) are two competing conceptions of democracy. The centralizers represent what has been referred to as the "elite" conception of democracy, wherein elites formulate and exercise governmental prerogatives and popular participation is restricted to the periodic selection of elites. This conception has guided constitutional choice, both in theory and practice, throughout most of the twentieth century. However, implicit in the position of Haley and Young is a profound, but frequently neglected, alternative conception of democracy that can be termed the "developmental" conception (Held 1987; Macpherson 1966, 1977, 1981; Pateman 1970). Although Haley and Young did not fully articulate this conception of democracy, it is articulated in the political thought of Jean-Jacques Rousseau, John Stuart Mill, Karl Marx, John Dewey, and Mohandas K. Gandhi.[5]

From the perspective of this tradition, human development rather than efficiency is the ultimate standard upon which systems of governance should be chosen and evaluated. Development, in this tradition, is conceived broadly as the all-around growth of the individual, which may include the development of moral, intellectual, spiritual, and creative capacities. The above theorists maintain that the realization of this value is contingent upon active participation in the decision-making processes of institutions.

The central thesis of this book is that the developmental conception of democracy provides the theoretical foundation for articulating an alternative model of school governance devoted not to the efficient integration of students into a hierarchical labor force, but to their development as unique human beings. Before proceeding to the main project of articulating a participatory system of school governance, it is important to discuss a number of assumptions that underlie, and perhaps justify, a developmental approach to the design of school governance.

First, an education devoted to the unique development of every student cannot be premised upon a model of teaching viewed as a routine technology demanding bureaucratization, rather such an education is premised on a conception of teaching as fluid and complex. From a developmental perspective, student needs and learning styles are diverse and demand that teaching be fluid. From this perspective, teaching is a creative rather than a routine activity, more like an art form than a rationalized technology. Being creative, it is based upon an integration of the conception and execution of instructional and curricular strategies, just as art is a manifestation of the artist's mental image. This view of teaching necessitates an organizational structure that directly involves teachers in the formulation of educational policy. If teaching is a fluid, complex, creative act, then a bureaucratic system of governance that disallows teacher participation in the policy process will undermine their professional development, in essence de-skilling them. This proposition is supported by the empirical finding of a significant relationship between decisional deprivation (lack of teacher participation in the decision-making process) and teacher alienation (Johnston and Germinaro 1985; Mohrman et al. 1978). It has become quite apparent that bureaucratic organization profoundly inhibits the development and expression of creative capacity. Bureaucratic rationalization is alienating.

Second, it is also apparent that if students are going to develop and flourish, parental involvement in their education and their schools is critical (Becker and Epstein 1982; Cattermole and Robinson 1985; Epstein 1986, 1987; Rich, 1985; Walberg 1984). Parents are primary care-givers and thus are the "guardians" of the interests and well-being of their children (Swanson 1989). Such guardianship entails a vision of the broad aims of the child's education and an understanding of the relationship between goals and methods. For example, parents may envision a college education for their child but may not realize that placement in vocational education could undermine that achievement. The vision of aims and an understanding of the relationship between those aims and curriculum and methods in turn entails critical reflection. Parents must be able to discriminate between what is and what is not in the developmental interest of the child. Therefore, the development of the parent's capacity to reflect critically on educational aims and their relationship to curricular and instructional policies is essential. The developmental conception of democracy, discussed in detail in chapter 2, maintains that participation in the decision-making processes of institutions provides an unique environment for the development of critical reflection and judgment, for such participation entails active inquiry, communication, and moral sensitivity (see also Sirotnik and Clark 1988). Therefore, parental participation in school governance could enhance the quality of their involvement in the education of their children (in terms of judgment and commitment), thereby facilitating the educational process.

Third, leadership in schools is also essential if schools are to be effective developmental sites (Bridges 1967; Erlandson and Bifano 1987; Lortie 1975; Miskel and Gerhardt 1974; Rutherford 1985). However, there are many different conceptions of leadership. Leadership consistent with the developmental ideal is conceived here as an interactive process between leaders and followers that has a transformative and empowering effect on both, rather than a process wherein leaders get others to follow their directives and subscribe to their points of view (Foster 1986). The latter emphasizes efficiency and control; the former, participation and development. The former is based upon Burns's (1978) notion of "transformational leadership." Transformational leadership does not merely seek to fulfill the goals of followers or to fulfill the goals of leaders through bargaining, what Burns terms "transactional leadership." It attempts to transform them, wherein "both leaders and followers are raised to more principled levels of judgment" (Burns 1978, 455). The leader's role is essentially "consciousness raising on a wide plane" (Burns 1978, 43). Following Burns, Warren Bennis observes that the essence of transformational leadership is "the ability of the leader to reach the souls of others in a fashion which raises consciousness, builds meanings, and inspires human intent that is the source of power" (1984, 70). Along with Bennis, Foster expands Burns's notion of transformational leadership by adding "power" into the equation. Foster argues that developing one's followers to a higher level of judgment is incomplete without also empowering them and making them into leaders themselves.

> Leadership is not manipulating a group in order to achieve a preset goal; rather it is empowering individuals in order to evaluate what goals are important and what conditions are helpful. The educative use of leadership results in the empowerment of followers. The leader here is truly concerned with the development of followers, with the realization of followers' potential to become leaders themselves (1986, 185–186).

Leadership is conceived here not in terms of control, but rather in terms of guiding others to higher levels of judgment and self-governance. Critics of participative decision making in schools (e.g., Geisert 1988) argue that participation will undermine the administrator's ability to lead. If leadership is defined as control, there is no doubt that such leadership will be significantly impeded by participative decision making. If leadership is defined in terms of transformation, however, then it will be profoundly enhanced by a participative system. From this perspective, the participation of others does not contradict the professional development of administrators, it is a necessary condition for it. Administrators as transformational leaders play an essential role in creating a developmental environment in schools. Through such leadership, deliberation, critical reflection, and judgment of teachers and parents can be facilitated.

Fourth, as a public institution the school is subject to larger community interests, some of which—for example, the reproduction of a hierarchical labor force benefiting corporate interests as indicated by the research of critical scholars (e.g., Bowles and Gintis 1976; Apple 1979, 1982)—contradict the developmental ideal. If the school is to become a developmental site for all students, the values and attitudes of significant portions of the community must change. Based upon the tenets of the developmental conception of democracy (chapter 2), it is hoped that, through participation in collective deliberation concerning the broad aims of public education, individuals intent on using the school to fulfill their own private interests will become aware of the common interest that unites the entire community. If the society is to flourish as a genuinely democratic community, each future citizen must be given the opportunity to develop their full and unique potential through the educational experience. The proposition here is that new values will emerge through collective deliberation, perhaps a transition from competition and greed to solidarity and concern that will give rise to a general commitment to schooling as primarily developmental.

Finally, the question exists whether participation in school governance, at least for high school students, constitutes an important dimension of an education devoted to the liberation of every student's full potential. Is participation essential for a genuinely "liberal" education? Of course, the answer depends upon one's philosophical conception of liberal education. Liberal education has its origins in Greek culture. The highest aim of Greek culture (*paideia*) was the formation of the ideal man, the cultivation of human excellence (*arete*). For the Romans, the inheritors of Greek culture, this cultivation or *paideia* was described as *humanitas,* from which we derive the notion of the humanities or the liberal arts. In its original formulation, liberal education thus liberates the full value of humanity, enabling one to be a free, self-governing human being (Jaeger 1953, 1965). Although Greek and Roman liberal education were devoted to the development of human excellence, the ideal of human excellence was contested, which generated two competing conceptions of liberal education: the philosophical and the democratic traditions of liberal education.

The philosophical conception of liberal education is "an education based fairly and squarely on the nature of knowledge itself" (Hirst 1973, 88). This conception is based upon the metaphysical and epistemological tenets of a realist theory of universals. This theory maintains that universals exist independently of human minds and these universals form the essence of particulars in the world (Woozley 1967). Plato's idealism may be the quintessential example of this theory in Western thought. Knowledge, in turn, is the product of the direct apprehension of universals that orders and fulfills the mind, constituting the excellence (virtue) of the mind. Thus, a classical realist views a liberal education based upon the pursuit of knowledge for its own sake "as freeing the mind to function according to its true nature, freeing reason from error and illusion and freeing man's conduct from wrong" (Hirst 1973, 89).

This epistemological conception provides the basis upon which the whole educational enterprise is patterned (Hirst 1973). For example, in Plato's epistemology, as represented in the *Republic* by the divided line and the allegory of the cave, the achievement of knowledge constitutes a movement from concrete, sensory experience to abstract, rational (intuitive) cognition, described by Plato as a process of "turning. . .the whole soul and its organ of learning [reason] away from becoming until it faces being and can endure contemplating the brightest of what is" (1979, 518c–d). The progression in Plato's educational design, as described in the *Republic,* from gymnastics and poetry, to military training and arithmetic, to harmonics and mathematics, and eventually to the dialectic, is an attempt to turn the power of learning systematically away from appearance toward reality. Thus, the classical realist position provides a harmonious and hierarchical structure of knowledge upon which to pattern education, a progression from concrete to increasing levels of abstraction.

If we reject the realist theory of universals, however, then the conception of liberal education based upon knowledge for its own sake, the philosophical tradition, loses its justificaton.[6] Hirst attempts to rescue this notion by basing liberal education not on classical realism, but on conceptual realism. He argues that to have a "rational" mind "implies experience structured under some form of conceptual scheme" (1973, 97). We are able to gain understanding of both the world and our own internal mental states because we share a common conceptual scheme with others. Experience becomes intelligible through the public sharing of symbolic systems.

From this perspective, education is a process of engaging with various heretofore-unknown conceptual schema in the form of paradigm examples of a variety of disciplines of knowledge. In theory, this exposure would expand the mind by enlarging the symbolic systems through which we can more readily interpret and understand ourselves and the world. To undergo education is then "to learn to see, to experience the world in a way otherwise unknown, and thereby to have a mind in a fuller sense" (Hirst 1973, 98). Thus, liberal education, based solely on the nature of knowledge itself, is still possible if we define knowledge in terms of conceptual schema organized around empirical experience rather than as apprehensions of ultimate reality.

Based upon the understanding provided by the sociology of knowledge and the history and philosophy of science, however, knowledge is not solely conceptual. It is also sociopolitical in the sense that it is influenced in significant ways by power and structural relations (Berger and Luckman 1966; Boggs 1984; Kuhn 1970; Mannheim 1957). As Mannheim suggests, "there is a correlation between the economic structure of a society and its legal and political organizaton, and. . .even the world of our thought is affected by these relations" (1957, 137). From this perspective, all forms of knowledge are "ideologies" in the sense of being conceptual schema profoundly shaped by the collective life of the society (Apple 1979; Mannheim 1960; Zeitlin 1987).[7] The inference is that if all forms of knowledge are ideologies embedded in and influenced by the collective life of the society, than a liberal education based upon knowledge so defined must take into account this collective life. This leads to the "democratic" tradition of liberal education.

Werner Jaeger argues that "any future humanism [liberal education] must be built on the fact of all Greek education—the fact that for the Greeks humanity always implied the essential quality of a human, his political character" (1965, xxvi). For the Greeks, human nature was political, and thus liberal education was viewed as a preparation for life in the polis. More fundamentally, however, political participation was viewed as an essential part of liberal education itself. As Jaeger put it, "to the Greeks a general education meant a political education" (1953, 9). In this sense The Greeks originated the developmental conception of democracy. As Cynthia Farrar maintains, "the experience of being a member of a self-governing citizen body was a process of individuation" (1988, 6). This political dimension is what, according to Jaeger, accounts for the greatness of Greek education and the Greek mind: "the fact that it was deeply rooted in the life of the community" (1965, xxv).

The implications for liberal education are profound. From this perspective, liberal education would be comprised of a dialectic between lived culture and direct participation in community affairs and exposure to critical perspectives concerning various forms of knowledge. Given the fact that the school is one of, if not the, primary polis of the student, critical analysis of the social relations of the school and their connection to the larger society would be a necessary part of such education, which would be greatly enhanced by the direct participation of students in the affairs of the school, including its governance. In addition, and perhaps more important, students would be exposed to and engaged with adults in a meaningful and important activity, a crying contemporary need. As Harold Howe (1991) among others—for example Wendell Berry (1987)—point out, the gap between adults and young people has widened significantly to the detriment of the development of maturity, judgment, and responsibility of children and youth. A participatory system of school governance could be one way of increasing meaningful interaction between adults and students. The school would become a democratic polis with increased opportunities for the liberal development of the student.

To do justice to these five developmental assumptions would require a book-length treatment. They are offered here, however, as premises which underlie a developmental approach to the design of school governance. In this sense, this book is a thought experiment which asks, through the lens of constitutional choice, If development is our guiding value and participation is a principle consistent with that value, what other principles and what design features are consistent with development and participation as they apply to school governance?[8]

Chapter 1 provides an overview of the Chicago debate concerning school governance in the Progressive Era. The position of historical indeterminance and the reality of resistance is advanced, entailing an argument for the viability of developmental, as opposed to elite, democracy. Chapter 2 provides the theoretical articulation of the developmental conception of democracy as expressed in the political thought of Rousseau, Mill, Marx, Dewey, and Gandhi. A theoretical justification for developmental democracy is provided, as well as the articulation of developmental principles and design features. Chapter 3 articulates alternative design structures and decision rules for restructuring school governance premised upon the value of development. Chapter 4 provides a comparative analysis of the developmental theory and model of school governance with the current school-based management/school restructuring reform movement.

The theory and model of school governance offered herein attempts to provide alternatives consistent with the imperatives of human development. As a theory and model it constitutes more of a broad outline than a fully specified system of governance. Full specification, I believe, can only be achieved by participants in a process of pragmatic experience. I hope, however, that such participants will find the blueprint I offer helpful in the process of restructuring school governance.

1

Administrative Reform in the Progressive Era: The Chicago Debate

Between 1890 and 1920, every major school system in the industrial north underwent administrative reform. This reform movement was designed to produce maximum efficiency and social order. To achieve these ends, the movement sought to centralized decision-making power in the hands of powerful superintendents and small, citywide school boards comprised predominantly of successful business and professional men. A bureaucratic structure was created that limited popular representation, insulating policymakers from the demands of working and lower-middle-class interests. Although premised upon "getting politics out of the schools," administrative reform actually exchanged one political structure for another. An essentially democratic system was exchanged for an autocratic one (Hays 1964; Tyack 1974).

The national debate over political structure in the Progressive Era constitutes one of the few clear instances of such debate in American educational history. This was especially true in the case of Chicago, where the Chicago Teachers' Federation (CTF) and its supporters articulated an alternative political theory to the one espoused by "administrative progressives" and "corporate liberals," which formed the philosophical basis of their twenty-year campaign in opposition to centralization (Hogan 1985; Tyack 1974).

The Chicago debate centered on a conflict between two competing conceptions of democracy: the elite conception and the developmental conception. The purpose of this chapter is to examine the Chicago debate as a step, by grounding it historically, in articulating a developmental theory of school governance.

The Social, Political, and Economic Context of School Centralization

The school centralization movement was a part of a much larger social, economic, and political transformation that occurred between 1890 and 1920. The emergence of monopoly capitalism and its management philosophy, and municipal reform in accordance with this philosophy, profoundly shaped the school centralization movement.

Monopoly Capitalism

In response to the Great Depression of 1893–97, American industrialists moved to consolidate their firms into large corporations. This response was shaped by the nature of the depression. The Great Depression was precipitated by a deflation of prices, interest rates, and profits. The 1870s and 1880s saw rapid industrialization and productive output, but also intense competition. This competition resulted in a deflationary spiral that cut profits, endangering many firms (Hobsbawm 1987). The dominant view among industrialists at the time was that the consolidation of firms was necessary in order to "obviate the effects of competition" (Kolko 1963, 13). Charles Francis Adams, president of Union Pacific Railroad, characterized this view, "The principle of consolidation. . . is a necessity—a natural law of growth" (cited in Kolko 1963, 14, also note the proposition of historical inevitability implicit in this statement).

Consequently, although the Sherman Antitrust Act was enacted in 1890, rapid consolidation took place in the American economy between 1898 and 1904. Kolko points out that the antitrust legislation was enacted to regulate mergers rather than to prevent them. In 1895, only 43 firms disappeared due to mergers; however in 1898, 303 firms disappeared. In 1899, mergers peaked, with 1,028 firms disappearing. In 1900, 340 firms disappeared and 423 in 1901. From 1895 to 1904, an average of 301 firms disappeared annually, compared to 100 from 1905 to 1914 (Kolko 1963, 18–19). Consolidation was viewed as the primary way to reduce competition. It was a way to gain control over markets through oligopoly in order to insure a high rate of profit.

In addition, the consolidation movement was accelerated by the fact that huge profits were readily available for lawyers and investment bankers to put the new corporations together, like those profits garnered through hostile takeovers in the 1980s. For example, the House of Morgan made $150 million for putting together U.S. Steel (Kolko 1963). The high rate of profit available to promoters and underwriters of mergers added powerful momentum to the consolidation movement, irrespective of its capacity to achieve monopoly control.

Indeed, as Kolko points out, the control of the market through consolidation was limited, resulting in the need for governmental regulation of the economy. The mere size of the new corporations made them uncompetitive with smaller firms that arose out of new capital formations. Smaller firms were inherently more innovative than the large bureaucracies created through consolidation, which gave them greater adaptability to market fluctuations and made them more competitive. Without the ready ability to innovate, bureaucratic structures demand predictability; and predictability in the market place could be best ensured through governmental regulation of the economy. Consequently, corporate executives successfully lobbied for federal regulation through the establishment of such regulatory agencies as the Federal Trade Commission and the Federal Reserve Board (Kolko 1963). In the process, a precedent was set for government regulation of the private sector; classical liberal economic theory and practice was replaced by corporate liberalism. This precedent not only legitimized the centralization of economic authority, but it also legitimized the centralization of authority in other social realms as well, in particular public schooling. Corporate liberalism as a social philosophy legitimized the undemocratic centralization of power on all levels of society.

The Efficiency Movement

The size and complexity of the new corporations suggested to industrialists that traditional production methods and management systems were inadequate. A need arose for a "more rational or scientific way of controlling, monitoring and programming large and profit-maximizing enterprises" (Hobsbawm 1987, 44). This need was couched in the rhetoric of "efficiency," and a new management philosophy in its name emerged as "scientific management." As Hobsbawm notes, "The 'visible hand' of modern corporate organization and management now replaced the 'invisible hand' of Adam Smith's anonymous market" (45).

From 1890 to 1920 an efficiency craze hit the United States. One of the main preachers of efficiency was Frederick W. Taylor, whose system of "scientific management" gave concrete expression to the secular gospel. In general, scientific management was more a managerial philosophy than a practice in the sense that Taylor's complete system achieved only limited application, whereas its basic principles had a far-reaching impact (Montgomery 1979). As Bendix

(1963, 281) points out, "the social philosophy rather than the techniques of scientific management became a part of prevailing ideology." This philosophy can be summarized in terms of four basic principles:

1. centralized planning
2. systematic and detailed task analysis
3. detailed instruction and supervision
4. incentive wage payment systems (Montgomery 1979; Haber 1964).

Although some scholars tend to view the reorganization of work under scientific management as an inevitable result of the logic of technological development (e.g., Chandler 1977; Haber 1964), just as consolidation and governmental regulation were viewed as inevitable results of a competitive free market, others maintain that it was a strategy freely chosen in order to ensure a greater degree of control in an ongoing struggle between management and workers over production authority (e.g., Braverman 1974; Burawoy 1978; Montgomery 1979). The latter view is supported by Sabel and Zeitlin (1985), who argue that the emergence of mass production was not the inevitable result of the logic of industrial development, but that mass production was chosen among other alternatives on the basis of power considerations. They argue that there was a craft alternative to mass production as a model of technological advancement, that technologically vital firms on the economic periphery served as alternative models of production. Mass production and the use of rationalized systems of work organization (scientific management) were not inevitable developments determined by the march of economic history. They were strategies that management employed to usurp control of the production process in order to increase profits and undermine labor militancy.

Central to scientific management was the view that efficiency was contingent upon complete managerial control of production. Control, in turn was based upon knowledge, or as Braverman (1974) points out, the separation of the "conception and execution" of production. The judgment of the individual worker was to be replaced by the laws and principles of the job developed by management through time and motion study. Taylor's system was designed to usurp the knowledge dimension of the job and turn workers into mechanized implementors. In contrast to mass production techniques, where knowledge was centralized in the technology and organization of the assembly line, scientific management developed as a form of job organization, which centralized knowledge in the manager *qua* planner. If workers were reduced to mere implementors with a severely limited knowledge base, management would have complete control of the production process. From this perspective, efficiency was inseparable from control (Braverman 1974; Burawoy 1978; Edwards 1979; Montgomery 1979).

Some scholars (e.g., Braverman 1974) maintain that scientific management was successsful in its attempt to monopolize the knowledge base of production. A number of other scholars (e.g., Barrett 1983; Burawoy 1978; Edwards 1979; Montgomery 1979; Nelson 1975) maintain, however, that the workers' response to scientific management was not docility and obedience, but rather constituted attempts to articulate and apply their own versions of rationalization that would enable them to retain control of the production process. In reaction to the school centralization proposal, which was based upon the principles of scientific management, teachers articulated their own adminsitrative philosophy in an attempt to retain control of the educational process as well.

The managerial system based upon the principles of scientific management was not only conducive to managerial control of the production process, but it was also completely compatible with large-scale organization born of consolidation. As Hays (1980) points out, as the scope and scale of organizations increased, there was a tendency toward the centralization of decision making. Scientific management was in complete accordance with this tendency and it was present not only in business but also in municipal government.

Municipal Reform

The standard interpretation of municipal reform in the Progressive Era maintains that good government triumphed over the corrupt alliance of machine politicians and special interests. However, Samuel Hays provides a convincing argument for the view that municipal reform was motivated by the desire of business, professional, and upper-class groups to gain control of city government. "Reformers, therefore, wished not simply to replace bad men with good, they proposed to change the occupational and class origins of decision-makers. Toward this end they sought innovations in the formal machinery of government which would concentrate political power by sharply centralizing the processes of decision-making rather than distribute it through more popular participation in public affairs" (1964, 162).

Before the Progressive reforms, city government was comprised of "confederations of local wards, each of which was represented on the city's legislative body" (Hays 1964, 160). In this decentralized system, city councilmembers were representatives of ward interests, which usually were the interests of lower- and working-class groups. However, as the scale and scope of business firms grew, the ward system came under fire on the grounds that it did not pay enough attention to the city as a whole. Business growth demanded an infrastrucure that covered the whole city, including physical plant and social welfare concerns (Hays 1964; Tyack 1974). Hays argues (164) that the political corruption (graft) seen in this era was the result of powerful groups being denied access to formal power and not as the product of "evil men." In order to gain legitimate power, businessmen moved to reform the system by changing the structure of government and the selection of public officials.

Their model for reform was the business corporation. It was widely believed that government should be run like a business. Businessmen knew how to run large-scale organizations efficiently. As Haber points out, those who favored governmental efficiency "found scientific management a corroborative and invigorating idea" (1964, 116). Centralized authority in the hands of an administrative expert (city manager) or powerful mayor was in keeping with the tenets of scientific management and the interests of the business community.

Municipal reform generally took on one of three forms:

1. a commission plan where executive power was centralized in a board of five individuals;
2. city manager plans; and
3. city-wide election of city councils with strong mayoral power (mostly in large cities).

All of these forms centralized decision-making power, thereby limiting the influence of the majority of voters among the middle- and lower-income groups (Hays 1964), who, with the advent of large-scale immigration, were predominantly immigrants from Southern and Eastern Europe.

Municipal reform was a struggle between mutually exclusive systems of decision making: one decentralized and representative, the other centralized and autocratic. Whereas industrialists sought consolidation in order to gain control of markets and scientific management to gain control of the production process, municipal reformers sought centralization to gain control of the political system. Industrialists, promoters of scientific management, and municipal reformers all represented the same class interests, and their reforms were intended to serve those interests.

Urban School Centralization

Urban school reformers also sought a fundamental change in the structure and process of decision making (Tyack 1974), a change in keeping with the centralization movement in business and municipal government. Progressive reformers sought to "take schools out of politics" by shifting decision making upward and inward in hierarchical administrative systems (Tyack and Hansot 1982, 107). The conflicts of value, debate, and democratic representation were viewed as inefficient and unnecessary in a properly functioning system of school governance (Tyack 1974). The old, ward-based system of governance was viewed as based upon an outmoded village system where power was decentralized and contained in informal structures of representation that invite corrruption.

It was argued that decision-making authority should rest upon "scientific expertise" rather than political pull (Tyack and Hansot 1982). As was the case in business and government, this expert-based system was defined in terms of the principles of scientific management. For example, Harvey H. Hubbert, a wealthy member of the Philadelphia Board of Education, argued that it was only natural to apply the principle of corporate consolidation to education (Tyack 1974, 143). This meant centralized authority and precise standardization.

The principles of scientific management were adapted to school organization in three ways:

1. centralized planning (centralization of financial and educational policy decision making in the superintendent's office);
2. precise specification of curricula and lesson planning and standards of teacher performance; and
3. emphasis on the budget process as a planning tool (e.g., cost-benefit analysis) (Callahan 1962; Tyack and Hansot 1982).

This administrative structure was designed to turn teachers into educational workers who had no policy making authority. In the name of efficiency, which was supposedly based upon scientific understanding rather than arbitrary political power, the ward system that allowed significant degrees of representation and local control was destroyed. Control of the educational process shifted to educational administrators as representatives of certain class interests. For example, in Philadelphia, practically all the powers of the ward boards were abolished, and the central board was reduced from 42 to 21 members appointed by judges and chosen from the city at large rather than by ward. In New York, the ward boards were abolished, and the central board was reduced from 46 to 7 members. In San Francisco, authority was turned over to a bipartisan board of four directors appointed by the mayor and a citywide elected superintendent who was an ex-officio member of the board (Tyack 1974). In Cleveland, the board was reduced from 26 members and 3 paid executives to a seven-man council with one full-time executive director whose powers were wide-spread. Both the council and the executive director were to be elected in citywide elections (Cronin 1973). St. Louis reduced their board from 21 to 12 members and substituted citywide elections for ward elections. St. Louis also transferred authority for nominating professional staff to the superintendent, along with responsibility for curriculum, supervision, textbook selection, the suspension of teachers, and the selection of instructional clerks (Cronin 1973).

In all cases, reduced central boards, citywide elections, and the elimination of ward boards or ward representation paved the way for the concentration of power in the hands of superintendents. The reduced numbers of board members could not manage the affairs of expanding schools on a part-time basis. As Tyack (1974, 154) put it, consolidation created a "power vacuum" filled by educational administrators. It also effectively limited popular representation, giving control of school policy to business and professional elites. The overall result was centralized control in a corporate board with delegation of power to expert administrators (Cronin 1973).

In the final analysis, as Tyack points out, administrative progressives were not simply attempting to remove schools from politics; they were instead exchanging one form of political decision making for another. As was the case in municipal reform in general, a centralized, elite system replaced a decentralized, representative one. The system of governance proposed and erected by the administrative progressives is an example of what was later articulated as elite democratic theory. Its core features, centralized planning, precise specification of policy, and mayoral appointment of school board members, correspond directly to the core features of elite democratic theory: elite control of governmental prerogatives and a conception of participation limited to the selection of elites.[1]

Probably the clearest theoretical articulation of elite democracy has been put forth by Joseph Schumpeter in *Capitalism, Socialism and Democracy* (1942). Schumpeter defined democracy as "a political method... for arriving at political—legislative and administrative—decisions" (269). By "method," Schumpeter meant an institutional arrangement that would place decision-making power in the hands of a few individuals who had attained the confidence of the people. "Democracy does not mean and cannot mean that the people actually rule in any obivous sense of the terms 'people' and 'rule'. Democracy means only that the people have the opportunity of accepting or refusing the men who are to rule them.... Now one aspect of this may be expressed by saying that democracy is the rule of the politician" (284–285). The people in this system cannot be said to be engaged in self-rule, rather the people are nothing more than the "producers of government"; they are nothing more than a mechanism to select "the men who are able to do the deciding" (269).

Underlying Schumpeter's and the administrative progressive's conception of democracy is the view that relatively few people possess the intellectual ability or the education to pass judgment on public policy; expert control and bureaucratic administration are necessary in a complex world that demands scientifically informed judgments. In such a world, only "governments of experts" can manage public affairs (121–122). This view is essentailly Platonic, akin to a distorted notion of positive liberty as self-mastery (Macpherson, 1973), wherein it is maintained that rational elites must control the irrational masses in order for social order to be achieved.

This notion corresponds directly to Max Weber's (1946) concept of formal rationality embodied in bureaucratic organization. Weber believed that modern society demanded bureaucratic rationalization, characterized by hierarchical, centralized organization structures, formal rules, appointment of officals on the basis of expertise, and the division or specialization of tasks. Weber maintained that bureaucracy was the most efficient form of organization and efficiency and control were paramount in modern society. As Weber observes, "the bureaucratic organization... is, from the purely technical point of view, capable of attaining the highest degree of efficiency and is in this sense formally the most rational known means for carrying out imperative control over human beings" (cited in Reich 1988, 7).

In terms of democratic government, rationalization demands government control by elites. Widespread political participation is seen not only as being infeasible but also highly undesirable. A passive populace is viewed as optimal. As Seymour Martin Lipset notes, "The distinctive and most valuable element of democracy is the formation of a political elite in the competitive struggle for the vote of a mainly passive electorate" (cited in Arblaster 1987, 53). Sammuel Huntington (Crozier, Huntington, and Watannki 1975) argues that the rise of political participation in the 1960s constituted a "crisis of democracy." The crisis was constituted by the fact that widespread political participation was jeopardizing elite control, in turn jeopardizing rational control of society. Thus a passive public is "good" for "democracy," whereas an active, politically engaged public constitutes a crisis of democracy.

The democratic nature of this system is defended on the grounds that it is open, competitive, and accountable. Extensive empirical evidence suggests, however, that this system is highly undemocratic because elite decision-making positions are confined to a few individuals who do not compete with each other but who collude to maintain power. They are not publicly accountable in that the majority of key positions are not subject to election (Tozer 1987). Even if it were open, competitive, and accountable, an elite decision making system would be a very weak form of democracy if democracy is defined as "self-governance."

The Report of the Educational Commission of the City of Chicago (1898) was based upon the study of the Chicago school system and a comparative analysis of the reforms instituted in other cities. Due to its comparative perspective, the report summarizes thought about administrative reform in the Progressive Era. As Tyack (1974, 133) put it, the report constitutes "a compendium of centralist reforms." It is a clear statement of the philosophy of elite democracy and administrative centralization.

The Report of the Educational Commission of the City of Chicago

In 1897, Mayor Carter Harrison created a commission to investigate and report on the administration of the public school system of Chicago. He appointed William Rainy Harper, president of the University of Chicago, to the commission. The commission elected Harper as its chair, allowing him to exert a considerable influence on the commission's report.[2] Before his appointment to the commission, Harper had served on the Chicago Board of Education (nominated by the Chicago Civic Federation), and he had been the chair of the Chicago Civic Federation's committee on education (Hogan 1985; Murphy 1981).

The Chicago Civic Federation was the founding chapter of the National Civic Federation, an organization primarily of corporate executives, although they attempted to include labor leaders in order to influence the creation of a national labor policy. The federation's members, in keeping with the tenets of corporate liberalism, sought to regulate social life in order to ameliorate the excesses of the emerging corporate order and stabilize it. The National Civic Federation redefined liberalism from the removal of state control over private enterprise to state intervention in order to regulate the market economy (Weinstein 1968). Not surprisingly given Harper's connections to the Civic Federation, the commission's report was in keeping with the tenets of corporate liberalism.[3]

The Educational Commission of the City of Chicago reported that there were "grave defects in the present plan of administration" of the school system, and that it required "radical improvement." The fundamental defect was identified as "the administration of school affairs through committees of the board of education." This system had "proved on the whole unsatisfactory" (1898, xii). The commission argued that the committee system had resulted in "the appointment and retention of unnecessary and inefficient employees" in addition to "unwarranted difficulty and expense in the securing of school supplies" (xii). On the educational side, the committee system had been inflexible regarding reform of the curriculum, and teachers had been appointed and retained "in opposition to the recommendations of those who should practically determined all these questions" (xiii), that is, the Board of Education and its executives. In addition, there existed no salary schedule and no "plan of promotion" for teachers. All of the above were "vital defects" (xiii).

In 1879, the Illinois State Legislature enacted the "Act to Provide for the Appointment of School Directors and Members of the Board of Education." This act stipulated that the mayor of the city should appoint the members of the Board of Education from each ward of the city. In 1889, this stipulation was amended under the "Act to Establish and Maintain a System of Free Schools" for cities with populations fewer than 100,000. This act stipulated that members of the board of education of such cities should be elected (Article VI, section 2). However, section 17 stipulated that appointment should continue in cities with populations greater than 100,000. Chicago was the only such city in Illinois.

According to the Educational Commission of the City of Chicago (ECCC), the problem with ward representation was that each member of the board was committed to the interests of his constituents, to the neglect of the needs of the city as a whole (ECCC 1898, 10–11). It is important to note here that the constituents of the wards were primarily immigrant working-class individuals, whereas the interests of the whole city were defined by elite business and professional men as their own particular class interests. Thus, the concern here was to centralize authority in the hands of elite interests, "in harmony with the principle of concentration of authority and responsibility" (ECCC 1898, 6). The commission argued that "it is evident that a board can fairly represent a city as a whole with a much smaller membership than would be necessitated by representation from each ward" (11).

Representation of the city as a whole was based upon a "new conception of the functions" of the board (11). The commission conceived the board's function as being purely "legislative" rather than a combination of legislative and executive. It maintained that the board should be a broad, policymaking body, analogous to a corporate board of directors, which would have the responsibilty of prescribing "the general educational policy of the city" (14), including determining the curriculum and resource allocation. The separation of the legislative and executive functions of the board would attract "the very best men" (13) to serve on the board, that is, elite business and professional men. The "mass of detail work" inherent in committee management, which had kept these men from serving in the past, would be eliminated through the destruction of the ward system. Through citywide appointment (the size of the board would be reduced from 21 to 11 members) and the elimination of the executive responsibilities, an elite board could be ensured. Thus, the general educational policy of the city would be determined by corporate rather than popular interests.

The ward system had carried out its management functions through a number of committees comprised of representatives from each ward that managed the affairs of the schools in their respective wards. The commission argued that, with the rapid growth of the city, the committee system "had led to a very cumbersome and unwieldly system of administration" (24).

The commission proposed that the administration of the schools be delegated to a superintendent and a business manager. The 21 committees of the ward system would be reduced to 3 committees on educational, business, and financial affairs.

The commission proposed that the business manager be given control of the finance committee. It was proposed that he have the "charge and custody of the securities of the board and, under close supervision, act as its financial agent" (31). In addition, he was given the power to appoint "janitors, engineers and other persons whom he shall require to assist him in the business affairs of the board" (30), which had previously been subject to the "political pull" implicit in the ward system.

The superintendent was designated as the chief executive officer of the school system and would be "in full charge of both educational and business functions." He would be entrusted with the execution of policy "outlined only in general" by the board (25).

"Political pull," which meant popular representation, was viewed as the most serious problem facing the school system. The appointment and retention of teachers through personal influence of board members was cited as being profoundly harmful "to the living interests of the city" (35). The commission maintained that a system of supervision capable of eliminating political pull "must definitely and finally concentrate all authority in an officer [superintendent] who shall be weighted with responsibility" (35).

The commission proposed that the superintendent "be given a very large measure of power." They proposed that "as long as he possesses the confidence of the board, and is retained as superintendent, he should be left unrestricted and untrammeled in his efforts to establish and administer the schools along the lines of sound educational policy" (41–42). Thus, as long as the policies of the superintendent served the interests of the board of education, total decision-making power regarding business and educational policy would be concentrated in his hands.

Specifically, the commission proposed that the superintendent be given power to (1) "decide all questions that concern teachers and the teaching in the schools" (43); (2) determine "the course of study, the choice of text books and apparatus used in the teaching in the schools" (44); and (3) "promote or reduce teachers and fix their salaries...and dismiss any appointees" (43). In addition, they proposed that the superintendent have a seat on the board but no vote. They argued that he "is not to be considered an employee, but rather a worthy and honored co-worker with the board, and as such should be treated on equal terms" (48). In other words, the superintendent was to be considered a member of the corporate elite, a major breakthrough in status and power. It is no wonder, as Hogan (1985) points out, that successive Chicago superintendents (e.g., Benjamin Andrews and Edwin Cooley) diligently worked through administrative fiat to implement the provisions of the report despite strong opposition and the absence of legislative sanction.

The commission suggested that the most fundamental of all the questions affecting the schools was that "of securing a good force of teachers" (60). The superintendent was given the power to appoint teachers, however the commission argued that in large cities it would be impossible for the superintendent to "form a correct judgment of the mass of candidates through personal investigation" (62). They proposed the establishment of an "examining board" to assist him in this matter. This board would be comprised of three special examiners, one assistant superintendent, and the superintendent who would serve as chair. The examining board would be responsible for the appointment and promotion of teachers. Concerning the latter, a "rational method of promotion" (75) was proposed, wherein promotion was based upon past teaching success and professional advancement in terms of scholarship and teaching ability, determined by the report of the principal and superintendent of the teacher's district and "careful examination and approval of the examining board" (75).

A schedule of salaries was proposed based upon distinctions regarding "the grade or subject in which the teacher gives instruction, the term of service of the teacher, the success already achieved, and advance in scholarship and teaching ability" (76). In other words, salary increases should not only be based upon length of service, but also upon the difficulty of instruction, the degree of "efficiency" already shown, and evidence of scholarship.

In addition, the commission proposed that, in order to attract men into the teaching profession, especially in the higher elementary grades, "higher salaries be provided for men than for women in these grades" (78). The commission maintained that "paying higher salaries to men than to women of the same ability and training is not an unjust discrimination. The superior physical endurance of a man makes him . . . more valuable in the school system. Moreover, this question is a plain case of supply and demand" (80). It was felt that increasing the number of male teachers was essential for decreasing the high dropout rate of males in the upper elementary grades, and their numbers could be increased by offering higher salaries.[4]

Thus, the nature of the proposal contained in the report was consciously shaped by the *"ruling idea of concentration of authority and responsibility"* (56, emphasis added). In accordance with the managerial and social philosophy of scientific managment and elite democracy, decision-making power was centralized in the hands of an "expert" planner, the superintendent. Educational policy would be determined by the superintendent and his assistants, and the teachers would become mechanized implementors with no decision-making power. In this sense, the report embodied the principle of the separation of "conception and execution," the core of scientific managment. The report also embodied the principle of centralized authority as it was applied in municipal reform. A decentralized ward system of government allowed policy to be determined by a collection of interests, primarily dominated by working-class interests. With the rise of monopoly capitalism and the emergence of citywide interests, elite business and professional groups, notably the Civic Federation, moved to usurp political power from the dominant lower-middle and working-class element of the city. The proposal to eliminate ward representation on the board of education and the committee management system was consistent with municipal reform in general. The commission, backed by the Chicago Civic Federation, moved to insulate decision-makers from popular interests, thereby ensuring that educational policy would be shaped in accordance with corporate interests. The Progressive Era was the age of consolidation and the centralization of authority; Chicago was no exception.[5]

However, the commission was not naive. Its members knew that their proposals were autocratic and would meet strong opposition from teachers and the general public. As stated, "When larger powers are placed in the hands of a superintendent...there is distinct danger that the schools will fail to respond fairly to the ideal of the people" (140). Their concern, however, was not that democratic ideals were being violated, but that if public opinion was ignored, a strong dissatisfaction would arise that might "lead to radical changes through the appointment of new members to the board of education" (140). In other words, if a mechanism for entertaining public opinion was not established, elite hegemony would be threatened. Consequently, the commission proposed the establishment of two advisory councils.

The first advisory council was a community commission made up of six residents of a given district who would visit and observe each school in the district and report to the board of education regarding "the work of each school, the discipline, sanitary and other arrangements of the building" (142). Note the conspicuous absence of issues directly related to educational policy (e.g., curriculum, instruction, and placement).

The second advisory council was the proposed establishment of faculty councils made up of teachers in each school and district, with a general council for the whole city. These councils would be given the "right of direct recommendations to the board on all matters connected with the educational system of the city" (167).

Both advisory councils were designed to account for public opinion without handing over decision-making power. Teachers and residents were allowed to make recommendations, but they played no formal part in the policymaking process.[6] These councils were far less democratic than committee management; however, they provided a needed "democratic" veneer to the autocratic system proposed by the commission. This is an example of an attempt to "manufacture consent." Schumpeter argues that manufacturing consent is an essential, unavoidable element of elite democracy.

Human Nature in Politics being what it is, [elites] are able to fashion and, within very wide limits, even to create the will of the people. What we are confronted with in the analysis of political processes is largely not a genuine will but a *manufactured will.* . . .The ways in which issues and the popular will on any issue are being manufactured is exactly analogous to the ways of commercial advertising. . .in reality [the people] neither raise nor decide issues but. . .the issues that shape their fate are normally raised and decided for them (1942, 263–264, emphasis added).

Both Schumpeter and the commission maintain that the manufacture of consent is an inevitable fact of modern political reality and a central element of elite democracy (see also Herman and Chomsky 1988).

Not surprisingly, the report received wide-spread praise from a number of university presidents, scholars, and other educational administrators. For example, Nicholas Murray Butler, professor at Columbia University and editor of the *Educational Review,* observed, "I can scarcely restrain my enthusiasm at the almost ideal nature of your report as it is outlined. The thoroughgoing way in which you have formulated the best ideas in city school administration is sure to prove of great benefit not only to Chicago but to many other cities of the country. . .I regard its conclusions and recommendations as almost unassailable, whether viewed from the standpoint of theory or from that of practice" (cited in Chicago Board of Education 1899, 155). And David Starr Jordan, president of Stanford University, wrote, "I find myself in entire agreement with the spirit of the suggestions and I believe that on such a basis it should be possible to bring the public schools of a large city to the highest grade of efficiency" (cited in Chicago Board of Education 1899, 155).

But to the dismay of administrative progressives and the Chicago Civic Federation, official attempts to enact the provisions of the report repeatedly failed. Legislation was defeated in 1899, 1901, 1903, 1905, 1909, 1911, and 1913. It took nearly twenty years before the report was enacted into law in 1917.[7] The opposition to the report was led by the CTF and its supporters, especially Margaret Haley and Ella Flagg Young.

The Chicago Teachers' Federation Alternative

The commission argued that administrative centralization was a natural consequence of urban growth, just as industrial consolidation had been viewed as the logical result of economic development. However, the "rationalization" of industry in terms of both technology (i.e., mechanization and mass production) and organization (i.e., scientific management) were not the inevitable results of the logic of industrial development. Rather, they were alternatives chosen in order to gain control of the production process. Workers, however, did not merely acquiesce to this attack on their traditional autonomy, but they put forth their own versions of "rationalization" that would enable them to retain control of production. Likewise, school centralization was not the inevitable result of the logic of urban growth. It was instead a strategy corporate elites and administrative progressives employed to usurp control of the educational process from teachers and working-class immigrants. Like workers in general, the teachers of Chicago and their supporters did not acquiesce to the centralizers. They waged a twenty-year campaign against centralization based upon a developmental conception of participatory democracy.

The Chicago Teachers' Federation (CTF) was founded in 1897 to secure wage increases in accordance with increases in the standard of living and tenure to provide economic security. Although founded upon bread-and-butter issues, the CTF was also concerned with issues of authority and governance. Its members led the political opposition against administrative reform (Hogan 1985; Reid 1982).

Margaret A. Haley, one of the founding members and leaders of the CTF, led the fight against centralization. Haley recognized that school centralization was not an isolated phenomena but a part of a general societal trend. "Two ideals are struggling for supremacy in American life today," she wrote in 1903, "one the industrial ideal, dominating through the supremacy of commercialism; the other ideal of democracy, the ideal of educators" (1903b, 4). She maintained that "the tendency in the field of education today is the same as the tendency in the commercial, the financial and the political world—that of concentration of power in one man or one set of men" (1903a, 6). She argued that the proposals of the Educational Commission were "fundamentally wrong," for they conferred on one man, the superintendent, "all the duties and powers naturally and necessarily inherent in the whole teaching force and the people" (1903a, 7). In other words, the commission proposed to centralize authority, which, according to Haley, was naturally diffused. Centralization, therefore, was wrong on the grounds that it undermined the "rights of the rank and file" to exercise decision-making authority. It set "aside the principles of democracy in the internal administration of schools" (1903a, 7). Echoing these concerns, the CTF warned that the commission's report would give the superintendent "autocratic powers unknown to the Czar of Russia," that it would institute a police system "like in Russia" (*Chicago Tribune,* September 29, 1899, 8).

Haley argued that due to the dominance of the industrial ideal, the centralization of power, there was a strong trend toward " 'factoryizing education,' making the teacher an automaton, a mere factory hand, whose duty is to carry out mechanically and unquestionably the ideas and orders of those clothed with the authority of position" (1903b, 2). Consequently, she maintained that teachers had "no more voice in the educational system of which they are a part then the children they teach" (1903a, 8). Of course, turning teachers into mechanized implementors was an essential feature of scientific management and elite democracy.

Haley (1915) attributed the movement toward centralization to the desire among the "financial feudal lords of America" to control the public schools. Profits were contingent upon producing an obedient labor force, and the schools were the primary means to that end. As Haley put it: "the selfish interest of the wealth classes depends upon the breaking down of the popular power" (1915, 1). Elite interests were contingent upon centralized authority.

In her autobiography, Haley summarized the struggle against centralization in terms of a battle between "the two great opposing forces of American life: the defenders and the exploiters of true popular government" (Reid 1982, 270). The battle over the control of the public schools of Chicago was not merely a fight for teachers' rights, but a fight to sustain the "cause of liberalism" (Reid 1982, 270), a fight for democracy itself.[8] She maintained that the teachers' struggle against autocracy was "as profound and as precious as the early struggles of the men who founded this nation" (Haley 1915, 1).

Haley not only viewed the centralization of authority as profoundly undemocratic, but also as highly impractical. In an often-quoted passage she maintained that the commission's report "provided for a superintendent who would need to be omnipotent as well as omnipresent in all parts of the system at all times, and capable of perfect justice, and that the only instance in history where there had been such a visitor on earth was nineteen hundred years ago and that he was crucified. . .the teachers of Chicago did not believe that if he returned to earth that he would come to Chicago by way of the Midway Plaisance [University of Chicago]" (Reid 1982, xx).

Through the use of sarcasm Haley made the point that urban growth demanded not the centralization, but the diffusion, of power. According to Haley, centralized authority was impractical in a large school system, a position directly opposite to the prevailing ideology of efficiency. Thus, according to Haley, school centralization was both undemocratic and inefficient.

Ella Flagg Young, who studied under John Dewey at the University of Chicago and became the first female superintendent of the Chicago school system under Major Edward Dunne's board,[9] was sympathetic to Haley and the CTF's fight against centralization. She also held many similar views regarding the nature of the commission's report. In addition, she articulated a plan for a decentralized system of school governance.

Young recognized, as did Haley and the CTF, that the key to centralized authority was "close supervision" of the teaching force. She maintained that "no more un-American or dangerous solution of the difficulties involved in maintaining a high degree of efficiency in the teaching corps of a large school system can be attempted then that which is effected by what is termed 'close supervision' " (Young 1901, 107). Close supervision, in accordance with the tenets of scientific management, meant detailed instruction and standardization of all facets of the teaching process. It meant that all educational decisions would be made by the superintendent's office; teachers would merely implement the policy of that office. Young argued that this centralization of authority would turn teachers "into a class of assistants, whose duty consists in carrying out instructions of a higher class which originates method for all" (107).

Young saw the centralization of authority as a profound threat to the effectiveness of the school system. She maintained that "the level of power in the educational system is determined by the degree in which the principle of cooperation is made incarnate in developing and realizing the aim of the school" (9–10). In other words, school

effectiveness is contingent upon mutual cooperation between all
members of the faculty and administration. Central to cooperation
is the notion of freedom. Young (34) maintained that "freedom is an
essential" for effective teaching. For genuine cooperation to occur and
for a high quality of teaching to take place teachers must possess
"freedom of thought" (107). If every aspect of educational policy is
dictated by a central authority, then the very essence "of that form
of activity known as the teacher" is undermined (34). Without a "free
play of thought," there can be no genuine teaching and learning.

Young argued that freedom of thought was contingent upon the
existence within the school system of "organizations for the
consideration of questions of legislation" (107). She called for the
organization of school councils consisting of "every teacher and
principal" (108). Each school would have a council and would elect
delegates to a central council. The function of these councils would
be legislative. They would make policy recommendations to the
superintendent and debate disagreements through a deliberative
process. The system would enable teachers to have a voice in the
determination of policy through a free discussion of educational ideas,
wherein the "voice of authority of position" was absent.

Young acknowledged that the commission's report did provide
for "teacher councils" that could make recommendations to the
superintendent and the board, but she recognized the limitations of
the commission's conception. The commission's councils would be
limited to making recommendations without the capacity to debate
disagreements with the administration. Access to policy debate is an
essential feature of a democratic system of governance (Fishkin 1991).
Young maintained that by providing an organizational mechanism
that would give teachers access to information and the capacity to
debate issues openly with the administration teachers' freedom would
be preserved. The tendency to centralize authority would be checked
by a decentralized federation of teachers' councils. However, even
though Young provided teachers a voice and a means to participate
in the policy process, her proposal did not go far enough; it did not
provide teachers and parents with formal decision-making power. They
were allowed to debate policy, but decision-making authority still
remained the prerogative of the superintendent.[10]

However, Haley and Young do provide an alternative conception
of democracy. Implicit in their response to the administrative
progressives is a conception of democracy based upon the value of
human development. Haley and Young opposed centralization on the

grounds that disallowing teachers from participation in the policy making process would undermine their development as teachers, as well as undermine the educational process. They wanted a democratic system of governance, in part because such a system would be most conducive to their view of teaching as a fluid, complex, and creative act. From this perspective, a participatory system of school governance was justified on the grounds of being consistent with teaching as creative and being necessary for the further development of such teaching.

In summary, the elite theorists and the Education Commission of the City of Chicago argued that elite control is necessitated by the efficiency demands of modern society. The argument in this chapter has been that elite control is not inevitably tied to modernity, but it was "constitutionally" chosen. Haley and Young provide a historical precedent for an alternative vision of constituional choice: choice made on the basis of development rather than efficiency. This alternative was not formulated clearly or extensively by Haley and Young. However, it does have a significant philosophical tradition, to which we now turn.

2

The Developmental Conception of Democracy

The purpose of this chapter is to articulate the developmental conception of democracy as exemplified in the political thought of Jean Jacques Rousseau, John Stuart Mill, Karl Marx, John Dewey, and Mohandes K. Gandhi. Although the ideas of these theorists are divergent in many ways, representing a continuum of political thought from liberalism to socialism to anarchism, there is a common thread: they all maintain that human development should be our guiding value in exercising constitutional choice and that the realization of the developmental ideal is contingent upon participation in the policy making processes of the social institutions in which one has membership. I will not provide a comprehensive account of each theorist's political philosophy, but rather I intend to bring to light the centrality of development and participation in their political thought. These theorists provide classic articulations of this conception from a variety of political and cultural perspectives. Thus, they are taken to be representative of this view of democracy.[1]

Jean Jacques Rousseau

At the core of Rousseau's political philosophy, as embodied in *The Social Contract,* is his conception of human will. He maintains that there are three different kinds of will:

1. the "private or particular will" of the individual, which predominately tends toward one's own personal advantage;
2. the "corporate will," which is the will of those who exercise governmental perogatives (i.e., the prince); and
3. the "general will," which takes into consideration the common interests of the people as a whole (Rousseau 1973, 213).

The general will is not a mere aggregate of the private wills of the individuals who make up a society, it is the common interest they share as an association. As Rousseau asserts, "There is often a great deal of difference between the will of all and the general will; the latter considers only the common interest, while the former takes private interest into account, and is no more than a sum of particular wills" (1973, 183). In other words, "what makes the will general is less the number of voters than the common interest uniting them" (1973, 187).

Implicit in any form of human association is a shared or common interest. People form groups because they share something in common. The formation of associations is what Rousseau refers to as the "social contract." It is an agreement among individuals to form a collective body. According to Rousseau, "There is only one contract in the State and society, and that is the act of association" (1973, 263). The social contract is not a political contract between subjects and rulers, or the people and their representatives as is the case in Hobbesian and Lockean political thought; rather it is social and concerns the agreement among individuals to associate in groups based upon shared interests.

Given the nature of human association, the general will or the common interest uniting the members of an association is sovereign; it is the authoritative standard upon which the policies and actions of an association are directed, the raison d'être of the association. It "constitutes Law" (183). If human association is based upon a shared, common interest, and if a particular interest dominates and policies are enacted to serve that interest, the true motive of human association is shattered. "If. . .the prince should come to have a particular will more active than the general will, and should employ the public force in his hands in obedience to his particular will. . .the social union would evaporate instantly, and the body politic would be dissolved" (1973, 212). In other words, "the moment a Master exists, there is no longer a sovereign and from that moment the body politic has ceased to exist" (1973, 182). Thus, in order to maintain genuine human association, the general will must be sovereign. Rousseau's conception of sovereignty is thus clearly different than the Hobbesian conception, wherein once the political contract is entered into, the state assumes total sovereignty.

In order for the general will to be sovereign, however, it must be explicitly known by the members of the association. Rousseau maintains that the sovereignty of the general will is contingent upon being "declared" by the people as a whole. Only then does it become law, and such a declaration is contingent upon knowing the general will. The common interest that unites the members must be known by all, or at least by an overwhelming majority, in order for the general will to be the guiding influence in the life of the association.

The question that arises at this point is, How can the general will be known? Rousseau maintains that the general will can only be known through deliberation in an assembly of the members of the association (239). It is through participation in public deliberation that the individual begins to recognize that there are interests beyond his private interest. The individual begins to recognize that he possesses a shared interest that creates unity with the other members of society. Thus, as a result of political participation the individual is educated to distinguish between private will (personal desires and impulses), and public will (Pateman 1970, 24–25). In turn, the process of becoming aware of the general will is the process of becoming a "citizen." The degree to which the individual is able to distinguish between the private and the general will is the degree to which he attains "citizenship." Thus, the principal function of participation in public deliberation is the development of citizens.

In this regard, Rousseau maintains that an innate capacity exists in every individual for growth. Our internal organs and faculties naturally develop to a state of maturity. Rousseau maintains that if our own natural inclinations were allowed to develop without restriction, we would achieve happiness and freedom (1979, 473). This is what he refers to as the "education of nature." However, even though happy and free, we would not be "virtuous," we would be "good without merit" (473). For Rousseau, virtue is "what is most precious to man" (473). Our capacity for virtue is what separates us from other animals, which if left in their natural habitats, are happy and free but not virtuous. The virtuous individual recognizes that private will may be in conflict with general will and forgoes private inclinations for the public good (473). Therefore, the development of a completely virtuous person is contingent upon the development of the individual, private will (the central project of *Émile*) and the development of the citizen (the central project of the *Social Contract*). As Rousseau points out, an individual cannot be developed as "man" and as a "citizen" simultaneously (89). Before a citizen is created the individual's capacity to discern private will must be developed, for without knowing private will, the common interest that unites all individuals with others cannot be known.

It is important to point out that although the general will is not an aggregation of private wills, the common interest is organically connected to the personal interests of citizens. Individuals enter into social contracts because they recognize that a commonality exists between their own personal interests and those of others. However, as citizens, they must forego those private interests that damage the common interest if they are to maintain the benefits of a genuine association. Although on the surface it seems as if Rousseau is advocating totalitarian submission of the individual to the state, the individual is freely consenting to forgo private interest for the sake of preserving the benefits of association with others. If the cost is too high, the individual is free to leave the association. In additon, as Pateman (1970, 26) points out, political participation also guarantees that freedom will be preserved, for individuals will possess equal legislative power. When viewed from this perspective, Rousseau's controversial statement that an individual may be "forced to be free" can be understood not in an authoritarian sense, but in the sense that if an individual is to be a citizen, then by definition he must exercise legislative power, that is, freedom.

According to Rosseau's educational plan, the individual should enter the public arena having a fully developed sense of private will. Through political participation the individual can then begin to develop a capacity to discern the commonality between personal will and the will of others and discriminate among those personal impulses that are and are not in accordance with this commonly shared interest. Thus, through political participation the mature individual *qua* individual develops as a citizen, thereby developing as a virtuous person. For Rousseau, the citizen constitutes the fully developed person, an individual of virtue, and this can only occur through political participation.[2] Therefore, in terms of constitutional choice, Rousseau's most cherished value is the development of the virtuous citizen, and the realization of this value is contingent upon the principle of political participation. What follows is a discussion of particular design features that Rousseau articulated and that are consistent with this value and principle.

Given the sovereignty of the general will, "the legislative power belongs to the people and can belong to it alone" (Rousseau 1973, 208). Rousseau maintains that the general will "when declared, is an act of sovereignty and constitutes law" (183). This declaration can, however, only occur in assemblies, wherein the general will becomes known (236). Thus, in its purest form, legislation is a direct declaration of the will of the people as a collectivity. As such, it cannot be represented, but must emerge from the collective deliberation of the people (241).

Although legislative power resides with the people, "executive power. . .can and should be represented" (241). Rousseau maintains that those who formulate legislation should be barred from the responsibility of executing it, for execution entails a focus on particular details, which impedes the appreciation of the general will. Thus, Rousseau advocates a separation of legislative and executive powers, the legislative residing in the people and the executive in their representatives as direct agents susceptible to immediate scantion and dismissal (245). "The dominant will of the prince [the government] is, or should be nothing but the general will or the law; his force is only the public force concentrated in his" (212). Therefore, "the depositories of the executive power are not the people's masters but its officers; that it can set them up and down when it likes, that there is no question of contract but of obedience" (245, obedience of executive officers to the people).

Rousseau, however, is not advocating the separation of powers as a means to political constraint as was the case for Madison and Hamilton. Rather, the separaton of powers for Rousseau is a means to guarantee that the people will develop as citizens, as individuals who possess the capacity to engage in responsible political action. If the people are bogged down with the details of executing policy, the resources necessary to engage in deliberation concerning the broader issues of the general will are likely to be depleted. Thus, the opportunity to develop as citizens will be profoundly diminished.

Within the legislative body Rousseau advocates consensual decision making. He suggests that "when in the popular assembly a law is proposed, what the people is asked is not exactly whether it approves or rejects the proposal, but whether it is in conformity with the general will, which is their will" (250). Conformity to the general will is determined by the degree of unanimity that is reached in the poplular assembly (249). The greater the unanimity, the greater the conformity to the general will. In most cases, a majority may be sufficient (250). However, "the more grave and important the questions discussed, the nearer should the opinion that is to prevail approach unanimity" (251). On the one hand, unanimity safeguards justice. On the other hand, it has a developmental function. Consensual decision making demands a greater degree of involvement among the participants than majority rule does. Consensus demands that underlying assumptions be identified in order to address and resolve conflict. This demand theoretically entails greater depth of participation than mere voting. Therefore, a consensual system provides a greater opportunity for development.[3]

Rousseau, however, maintains that such a participatory system could only be workable on a small scale. In large states, public assemblies and deliberation by all citizens is not feasible. Developmental democracy was limited by what has been referred to as the "size principle."[4] Rousseau maintains that participatory democracy must be restricted to small city-states, for he deems representation in any form as illegitimate.

Thus, according to Rousseau, the nature of human asociation necessitates the development of "virtuous citizens." In order for a genuine community to exist, each member must possess knowledge of the general will and act in light of this knowledge. If a group of individuals agrees to form an association, then, according to Rousseau, they must necessarily choose human development as their guiding value and political participation as their overarching principle. In terms of the decision-making process itself, first, according to the principle of participation, every member would directly participate in the decision-making process, and each member would possess equal decision-making power. Second, a legitimate decision would be constituted by the degree of unanimity achieved. That is, for a decision to be legitimate, consensus would have to be gained within the association. Third, the content of deliberation would be confined to broad policy concerns. In terms of the general framework of constitutional choice, the guiding value for Rousseau is human development, conceived in terms of virtue and citizenship, which is contingent upon the principle of political participation from which the design features of direct democracy, consensual decision making, and separation of powers are derived.

John Stuart Mill

The stated purpose of John Stuart Mill's most famous work *On Liberty* is a justification of civil liberty. His aim is to determine "the nature and limits of the power which can be legitimately exercised by society over the individual" (1947, 135). His proposal is that the exercise of power over the individual is only justified when it is exercised to prevent harm to others. However, the basis of Mill's project, to which he devotes more than half of his treatise, is the metaquestion: Why should we be concerned with preserving liberty? It is this question, rather than an analysis of the harm principle, that is of concern here.

Mill maintains that his argument for the preservation of liberty is not based upon an "idea of abstract right" wherein liberty is conceived as an end "independent of utility" (145). Rather, liberty is justified on the basis of its utility "in the largest sense," "grounded on the permanent interests of a man as a progressive being" (145). For Mill, utility is defined in terms of the fundamental impulse of man, which is not happiness or pleasure as the original utilitarians (James Mill and Jeremy Bentham) maintain but development. Liberty is justifiable because it is a necessary condition for human development. This argument makes sense of Mill's seemingly unusual epigraph to *On Liberty*: "The grand, leading principle, towards which every argument unfolded in these pages directly converges, is the absolute and essential importance of human development in its richest diversity."—Wilhelm von Humboldt. It is utility *qua* development that justifies preserving liberty. Here human development is the end and liberty the means.

Mill maintains that there are three kinds of liberty: liberty of thought and discussion, liberty of choice, and liberty of association. First, he argues that intellectual development is contingent upon freedom of thought and discussion. "Not that it is solely or chiefly to form great thinkers that freedom of thinking is required. On the contrary, it is as much and even more indispensable to enable average human beings to attain the mental stature which they are capable of. There have been, and may again be, great individual thinkers in a general atmosphere of mental slavery. But there never has been, nor ever will be, in that atmosphere an intellectually active people" (1947, 169).

Mill argues that only by being free to explore the implications of a thought to its final conclusions, even if the process ends in the recognition of the falsity of the thought, will truth be discovered. If one is not allowed to pursue all avenues of thought freely, then opinion remains unexamined, and the unexamined acceptance of prevailing opinion yields a mentally passive people.

Freedom from mental imposition, however, is not a sufficient condition for intellectual development. Freedom of discussion is also necessary. A free and open discussion of ideas wherein one's ideas are tested in opposition to contrary ideas is essential for the development of mental capacities. As Mill put it, "No wise man ever acquired his wisdom in any mode but this; nor is it in the nature of human intellect to become wise in any other manner" (155). Mill argues that discussion enables one to correct one's own opinion in light of the criticism of others. It is through the process of debate that both the weaknesses and strengths of a position can be revealed. Through repeated debate, ideas are tested and refined, yielding a learned, informed opinion. In addition, not only does one gain a semblance of wisdom, but also one develops the ability to reason, discriminate, and communicate; giving the capacity for further inquiry. Classical liberals generally view freedom as being contingent upon rationality: human liberty can only be achieved through the development and exercise of reason. Mill suggests the reverse, however: rationality is contingent upon freedom.

Second, freedom of discussion is interconnected with the liberty of association. If we are not free to associate with those individuals of our own choosing, then our freedom to discuss is thereby limited. Restriction on association is an effective way to limit debate, for those with opposing viewpoints are shut out. Therefore, liberty of association is a necessary condition for liberty of discussion.

Third, Mill suggests that "the same reasons which show that opinion should be free, prove also that he should be allowed, without molestation, to carry his opinions into practice at his own cost" (193). Freedom of choice for Mill is also a necessary condition for both intellectual and moral development. "The human faculties of perception, judgement, discriminative feeling, mental activity, and even moral preference, are exercised only in making a choice" (195–196). Adhering to the tenets of faculty psychology, Mill argues that intellectual and moral powers are like muscles in that their development is contingent upon being exercised. In the act of choice, participation in the decision-making processes that affect our personal and public lives, our mental and moral faculties are exercised and developed. He argues that the process of choice necessitates the use of "observation to see, reasoning and judgement to forsee, activity to gather materials for decision, discrimination to decide, and when he has decided, firmness and self-control to hold to his deliberate decision" (196). Mill suggests that if decisions are made for another, that person may be led in a good direction, that is "out of harm's way," but he asks, "What will be his comparative worth as a human being?" (196). The usurption of decision-making power from the individual, either through unexamined custom or the centralization of authority, will produce mental passivity.

For Mill, active, critical engagement in the thought and affairs of one's social mileu, including the decision-making processes of social institutions, is essential for the development of the human faculties of reason, moral judgment, discrimination, and self-control. Therefore, the preservation of liberty, the aim of *On Liberty*, is justified on the grounds that it is a necessary condition for human development.

In his most mature political work, *Considerations on Representative Government*, this developmental ideal is extended into the realm of government, wherein development and political participation are viewed as the foundations of legitimate government. Mill argues, along with other constitutional choice theorists (e.g., Madison and Hamilton), that "institutions and forms of government are a matter of choice" (1861, 11). However, choice is not unlimited. Mill argues that the distribution of power in any society is determined by its socioeconomic context, and therefore is not open to choice. Within a given social context, however, the organizational structures of government can and should be chosen (1861, 12).

After establishing the validity of constitutional choice, Mill asks what criteria should be used in choosing a form of government. He maintains that the "best government is that which is most conducive to Progress" (1861, 25). However, for government to be conducive to progress, two critieria must be met. Government must efficiently and effectively conduct the affairs of the community, what Mill refers to as the "business" of government. It must also, and more importantly, develop the virtue and intelligence of the people.

> The most important point of excellence which any form of government can possess is to promote the virtue and intelligence of the people themselves. The first question in respect to any political institutions is, how far they tend to foster in the members of the community the various desirable qualities, moral and intellectual... .The government which does this best has every likelihood of being the best in all other respects, since it is on these qualities, so far as they exist in the people, that all possibility of goodness in the practical operations of the government depends (1861, 30).

Implied in this quotation is the view that the moral and intellectual development of the people is the most important end of government, for such development constitutes progress. Mill rejects the hedonistic orientation of the earlier utilitarians while preserving utility as an ethical and political criterion. In the political domain, government, for Mill, was not merely an agency for increasing sensate pleasure and decreasing pain. Mill introduces a qualitative distinction concerning utility (Magdid 1989). He views the higher human functions of intelligence and virtue as superior pleasures. Thus, according to his modified utilitarianism, the development of these higher functions constitutes progress. In addition, the actual conduct of governmental business is conditioned by the general development of the people. The degree to which the government can operate efficiently and effectively is the degree to which the people as a whole are developed. Governmental agents do not act in a vacuum, but conduct their affairs in the context of public opinion, which can either support or undermine their actions (Mill 1861, 29–30). Thus, "a government is to be judged by. . .its tendency to improve or deteriorate the people themselves, and the goodness and badness of the work it performs for them and by means of them" (33).[5]

Given this developmental criterion for choosing a form of government, the question of which form meets this criterion arises. Or, in terms of constitutional choice, what political principles and design features are consistent with development? In order to answer this question Mill employs a thought experiment. If there existed an enlightened, benevolent monarch who, based upon his omniscience, could conduct the affairs of the community with utmost efficiency and effectiveness, would a government based upon such an enlightened despotism, wherein absolute power was located in one individual, be the ideally best polity?[6]

Mill argues that under such a regime the people would be "without any potential voice in their own destiny" (46). Everything would be decided for them, there would be no liberty of choice. The public would also be devoid of any information regarding public affairs; there would be no meaningful liberty of thought and discussion. Mill asks: "What sort of human beings can be formed under such a regimen? What development can either their thinking or their active faculties attain under it?" (1861, 47). Mill maintains that the nation would be composed of mentally passive people. A people morally and intellectually stunted, for the opportunity for discussion of meaningful, public issues would not exist. To a large extent mental faculties would not be exercised, and therefore not developed. In addition, following Rousseau, Mill argues that an opportunity to distinguish between one's own private desires and the common interest would not exist. Thus, one's moral sentiments would be confined to one's own private desires, never expanding to issues of greater human concern (Pateman 1970, 30). Without knowledge of the common interest, which can only be known through discourse with others concerning public issues, a standard upon which to judge the morality of private desire does not exist. In this situation, individual morality is "narrowed and dwarfed." Therefore, the centralization of power, even though benevolently exercised, is inconsistent with the developmental ideal, and hence illegitimate.

Implicit in this argument against an enlightened despotism, as was the case in Mill's argument for liberty, is the proposition that development requires active engagement, that moral and intellectual development is an active process. In order to be consistent with development, a system of government must be structured so that the people actively participate in its affairs, especially its decision-making processes. "From these accumulated considerations it is evident, that the only government which can fully satisfy all the exigencies of the social state, is one in which the whole people participate...that nothing less can be ultimately desirable, than the admission of all to a share in the sovereign power of the state" (1861, 69). Thus, Mill adhers to the political principle of participation as a means to the developmental end.

For Mill, the design specifications that follow from the principle of participation are limited by the constraints of a modern society. Ideally, every individual would participate in the formation of public policy. As both Rousseau and Mill point out, however, direct democracy is only possible on a small scale. Thus, Mill concludes that in a modern society "the ideal type of perfect government must be representative" (1861, 69). The size principle is not the only force driving Mill toward a representive system, however. Given its complexity, he also maintains that expertise in the formation and implementation of public policy is essential for effective and efficient government in a modern society.

Mill is willing to move to a representative system while still adhering to the developmental conception, for he believes that the process of election will necessitate active political participation and, more important, that individuals will have the opportunity to participate in the governance of local community affairs and other social institutions, including industrial organizations. Thus, although Mill's concern for competence and efficiency diminish his commitment to development, in compensation he is willing to extend participation to "non-governmental" realms, sites such as industry not normally considered to be open to democratic participation in order to remain consistent with the developmental ideal. Thus, although representation is a necessary evil in a modern society, the developmental end can still be served through participation in elections and, more importantly, through direct participation in local community and industrial affairs.

A number of inconsistencies remain, however. First, in spite of this position Mill restricts citizenship to those individuals who are literate and who pay taxes. In addition, those citizens deemed more "competent" are entitled to extra votes. Thus, decision-making power is unequally distributed. Concerning the national policymaking process, "citizens" elect representatives who engage in a ratification process. According to Mill a planning body comprised of competent experts appointed by representatives would engage in the formulation of national policy. Representatives would be charged with ratifying the decisions of the planning board. Second, representatives and their appointees are free to act independently of their constituents. For Mill, representation entails a grant of decision-making authority. Third, although Mill was deeply afraid of majority tyranny, decisions are to be rendered on the basis of majority vote. Given the proportional voting scheme, which unequally distributes decision-making power on the basis "competence," Mill's system is not a pure majoritarian system. Rather, it is a system that attempts to ensure minority rule while giving a voice to the majority. These design specifications are inconsistent with the developmental ideal.

Thus, Mill views liberty of thought and discussion, association, and choice as necessary conditions for optimal human development, conceived in terms of moral and intellectual development. Such development is the ultimate end of government. In the governmental realm, liberty of choice translates into the principle of political participation. To the greatest extent possible, individuals should directly participate in the formation of policies that affect their lives. In the same breath, however, Mill advocates the unequal distribution of decision-making power on the grounds of size and competence, thereby moving away from the developmental ideal. He presents a fundamental dilemma for modern developmental theorists. How can the need for expertise and the imperative of representation due to size be reconciled with the participative imperatives of the developmental ideal? (See synthesis below and Chapter 3.)

Karl Marx

In the first volume of *Capital*, Karl Marx writes:

We pre-suppose labour in a form that stamps it as exclusively human. A spider conducts operations that resemble those of a weaver, and a bee puts to shame many an architect in the construction of her cells. But what distinguishes the worst architect from the best of bees is this, that the architect realises his structure in imagination before he erects it in reality. At the end of every labour-process, we get a result that already existed in the imagination of the labourer at its commencement. He not only effects a change of form in the material on which he works, but he also realises a purpose of his own that gives the law to his modus operandi, and to which he must subordinate his will (Cited in Braverman 1974, 45–46).

Marx is arguing that what distinguishes human from animal production is that the former is based upon a consciously chosen purpose, whereas the latter is based upon instinct. Human beings possess the capacity to conceive their productive activities, to translate ideas into material forms. Marx maintains that while the animal produces only out of direct physical need, man "produces even when he is free from physical need and produces truly, indeed, only in freedom from such need" (1983, 139). This capacity of conscious production is the defining characteristic of human nature. For Marx, human nature is defined by the capacity to not only produce, but also to produce that which is consciously and freely chosen. Thus, the Marxian claim that humans are essentially creative beings has a distinctively purposeful, freely chosen, dimension (Braverman 1974; Cropsey 1989).

However, when physical need forces individuals to sell their labor power, and thus to execute the prerogatives of others rather than their own, their labor power becomes alienated from their nature as human beings (Marx 1983, 140). As Braverman points out, although in human affairs conception always precedes execution—which is precisely what makes them *human* affairs—the "unity of conception and execution may be dissolved" in the sense that an idea may be conceived by one individual and executed by another (1974, 50–51). If an individual is restricted only to the execution of another's prerogatives, then he or she is denied the opportunity to engage in human production. Labor power is reduced to animal production. As Marx put it: "Alienated labor. . .alienates from man his own body, as well as nature outside him, as well as his spiritual being, his *human* being" (1983, 140, emphasis in original). In the case of alienated labor the individual is dehumanized.

Therefore, in order to realize full humanity, to develop as a human being, an individual must at least actively participate in making decisions that will bear on personal action, if not fully decide them. Thus, in Marx's view self-determination via participation in decision-making processes is a necessary condition for human development. Consistent with the developmental conception of democracy, the measure of any sociopolitical institution is the degree to which it allows individual self-determination. "In democracy the constitution, the laws, the state itself as a political constitution is only a self-determination of the people. . . . It is self-evident. . . that all forms of state have democracy as their truth, and therefore untrue in so far as they are not democratic" (Marx 1983, 90). The truth or falsity of an institution is thus the degree to which it provides the opportunity to participate in its decision-making processes; self-determination is necessary for human development. For Marx, participatory democracy is mandated by the developmental ideal.

In popular U.S. culture, Marxian political thought is equated with the undemocratic centralization of power. The preceding argument suggests that this view is actually more a result of political propoganda than an accurate reading of Marx. The undemocratic political structures of the Soviet Union and the Eastern Bloc under communist rule were fundamentally Leninist (and Stalinist) rather than Marxist.[7] For example, Lenin was enamored with Frederick Taylor's scientific management. He wrote: "The Soviet Republic must at all costs adopt all that is valuable in the achievements of science and technology in this field [scientific management]. The possibility of building socialism depends exactly upon our success in combining the Soviet power and the Soviet organization of administration with the up-to-date achievements of capitalism. We must organize in Russia the study and teaching of the Taylor system and systematically try it out and adapt it to our ends" (cited in Braverman 1974, 12).

In fact, Lenin established the Central Labor Institute under the direction of Alexei Gastev to study scientific management and its application, not only to industry but also to the management of society. Gastev sought to extend scientific management to all spheres of life. He viewed society as a vast machine and its members as cogs in that machine. He viewed the worker as being deprived of all creative capacity, which meant the authoritarian control of labor. Lenin enthusiastically supported Gastev and the Institute, advocating a dictatorship in the workplace wherein authority would be concentrated in the hands of management. In order to achieve socialism, Lenin demanded an "increase in production at all costs" (cited in Sirianni 1982, 254). Democracy was dispensible. Thus, the initial democratic impulse of workers' councils at the outset of the revolution was destroyed by the authoritarian philosophy of Bolshevism, not Marxism per se (Arendt 1962). In contrast, Marx maintained that the complete realization of humanity was contingent upon the complete democratization of society.

Marx's historical model for this democratization was the Paris Commune. In 1871, a revolutionary uprising occurred in Paris in which workers sought to overthrow what they regarded as a corrupt governmental structure. The workers proposed a set of institutional innovations and a new governmental structure referred to as the "Commune." The Commune had a number of important features: (1) integration of legislative and executive functions; (2) decentralized governance of local affairs by municipal delegates elected by ward; (3) election of delegates to higher governmental bodies; (4) revocability of delegates; and (5) short terms of office (Marx 1983, 528).[8]

In Marx's view this structure allows individuals to control their own affairs. A key to this self-determination is decentralization, which provides accessibility to decision making. Another key is revocable delegation, wherein a delegate is bound to represent the will of the people. Revocability is an accountability mechanism in the sense that if the delegate strays from the mandate of the people, he can be immediately replaced. Election by ward ensures a close proximity of delegates to constituents, thereby also increasing representation. The combination of election by ward, decentralization, and revocable delegation provide an opportunity for the individual to participate directly in the policy making process. In this system it is the citizens as a collectivity who formulate public policy, for they are formulating the mandate the delegate is obligated to carry out. Delegation is therefore a means of resolving the conflict between decentralization and representation arising out of the size principle. Delegation is a compromise that allows for representation while safeguarding a significant degree of direct participaton (See Chapter 3). Thus, in Marx's view, the people would be self-governing, thereby exercising and developing their true nature as creative beings. "The Commune is the resumption of the authority of the state by society as its own living power instead of as a power controlling and sub-doing society; it is the resumption of authority by the masses themselves, forming their own power in place of the organized power of their oppression; it is the political form of their social emancipation" (Marx 1983, 528). Within this framework of collective decision making, Marx believed the "free development of each" would entail the "free development of all" (228).

However, a significant omission exists concerning the design features of the Commune. The question of "decision-rules" is never addressed. Marx naively assumes that consensus will exist automatically on each level of the communal system, for class divisions will be dissolved. However, conflicts exist within classes as well as across classes. It is certainly plausible that this reality would continue even if society was completely democratized. Therefore, as David Held suggests, "a series of institutional procedures and mechanisms for debating and taking decisions about public affairs is essential" (1987, 137). Marx fails to provide this essential, for he naively envisions an end to politics. Without decision-rules the communal system is susceptible to the usurption of policy by minority factions. Without procedures for the adjudication of conflict, power, rather than reasoned political debate, becomes the sole determiner of public policy. Participation and self-determination are then eliminated.[9]

Thus, Marx's conception of human nature as free and creative demands that individuals participate directly and with equal power in the decisions that affect their lives in order to develop as complete human beings. From this principle the communal model of governance outlined previously is derived. Marx's political thought is premised upon the developmental ideal and the principle of participation, extending their relevancy to all social institutions. He attempts to articulate design features consistent with these ideals in the form of the Commune. His communal model provides important insights into the structure of a developmental model in terms of decentralization and delegation as well as neglect of decision-rules.[10]

John Dewey[11]

In *Reconstruction in Philosophy*, Dewey asserted that utilitarianism had "acclimatized in human imagination the ideal of social welfare as a supreme test" (1948, 180). While accepting the utilitarian principle that moral questions should be decided on the basis of standards of welfare, Dewey, like John Stuart Mill, rejected the hedonistic standards of pleasure and pain of early utilitarianism in favor of the standard of "development" or "growth." Echoing Mill, Dewey maintained that the most fundamental value of classical liberalism has endured, "the development of the inherent capacities of individuals made possible through liberty" (1988, 123). For Dewey, the moral end to be achieved in both public and private life was growth. His whole conception of democracy, which formed the foundation of his philosophical system, was premised upon the developmental ideal.

Dewey's conception of growth was profoundly influenced by Charles Darwin. In Dewey's view, Darwin had "freed the new logic. . .for application to mind and morals and life" (1910, 8–9). In essence, this new logic consisted of the proposition that change entails the possibility of "novel and radical deviation,. . .of new possbilities and ends to be attained" (1910, 102). The classical liberals had believed that progress was inevitable. With the advent of Darwin, progress could no longer be viewed as such, for some species died out while others evolved. The key factors were the capacity of the species to adapt to environmental change and the nature of the adaptation being determined by the nature of the environment. Growth for Dewey was defined as adaptation (reconstructed experience) to environmental change (new experience), which results in "an enlarged and changed experience" tending toward the development of one's moral, intellectual, and physical capacities (1916, 5). Different environments will require different adaptations, which in turn will develop different faculties. However, not all environments are educative; some will retard rather then stimulate development. In general, growth is contingent upon active interaction with an educative environment.

Dewey argues that human beings are essentially social in nature. We are born and live our lives in association with others. Thus, human associations form our primary environments. Being primary, the quality of human association is the fundamental determining factor in our development. The quality and nature of social arrangements determine the moral and intellectual development of the individual. Dewey concludes that social "institutions are viewed by their educative effect: with reference to the types of individuals they foster" (Dewey 1948, 196). He argues that when considering the constitituion of a social institution, we should "ask what the specific stimulating, fostering and nurturing power of specific social arrangement may be.... Just what response does *this* social arrangement, political or economic, evoke, and what effect does it have upon the disposition of those who engage in it? Does it release capacity? If so, how widely? Among a few, with a corresponding depression in others, or in an extensive and equitable way?" (1948, 196–197, emphasis in orginal).

According to Dewey, the measure of a social institution is the degree to which it develops, in an equal and extensive manner, the intellectual and moral capacities of the individuals who comprise it. Dewey asserts that "such questions as these... become starting points of inquiries about every institution of the community when it is recognized that individuality is not originally given, but is created under the influences of associated life" (1948, 197). From Dewey's perspective, given the fact that character is socially constructed, human development should be the moral standard that determines constitutional choice. The question arises, What kind of social arrangements are conducive to development? Dewey (1927) maintains that optimal human development can only take place in social arrangements that possess a variety of common interests; free and extensive communication; and participation in the decision-making processes of group life.

In *Democracy and Education,* Dewey argues that the degree to which consciously shared interests are numerous and varied, and how free and fully the interaction with diverse forms of association is attained, will have a significant impact on development, for "these more numerous and more varied points of contact denote a greater diversity of stimuli to which an individual has to respond" (1916, 87). A greater diversity of stimuli will require the individual to adapt in numerous ways, resulting in a more extensively reconstructed experience. For example, mental powers that would be suppressed "as long as the incitations to action are partial" are liberated when exposed to diverse interests and forms of associaton (1916, 87). For example, belonging to a criminal band with only one interest, plunder, restricts rather than liberates one's full potential. In addition, the nature of manifold association and the richness of that association are interconnected in the sense that its richness is determined by the degree to which the numerous and varied interests are consciously shared. Interests may be manifold, but if they are not consciously shared, their power as stimuli is greatly reduced. Thus, the degree of commonality or community (i.e., consciously shared interests) constitutes the richness, and thereby the educative power, of association. Such commonality is, however, contingent upon both the quality of communication and the degree of participation in decision making.

Dewey maintains that in general the communicative act is educative for both the communicator and the listener. The listener shares in the thought and feeling of the communicator and is thus more or less influenced by him or her (1916, 5). However, the communicator is more directly affected, for "experience has to be formulated in order to be communicated" (1916, 5–6). This formulation requires self-reflection, imagination, clarity of thought, and sensitivity to the experience of others, all of which enlarge the experience of the communicator. Thus, Dewey concludes that communication "enlightens experience; it stimulates and enriches imagination; it creates responsibility for accuracy and vividness of statement and thought" (1916, 6).

In addition, communication has an implicit moral effect, for it is through acts of communication that one becomes aware of shared interests. Echoing Rousseau and Mill, Dewey argues that through communication one develops the capacity to distinguish between private desire and the public interest. With the development of this capacity, private desire is informed by public concerns (i.e., concerns that encompass the well-being of the social group in which one has membership), thereby increasing the ethical sensitivity of the individual. As Dewey suggests, moral community is created through "the perfecting of the means and ways of communication of meanings so that genuinely shared interest in the consequences of interdependent activities may inform desire and effort and thereby direct action" (1927, 155). Thus, communication is essential for moral and intellectual development. "The individual...except in and through communication of experience from and to others, he remains dumb, merely sentient, a brute animal. Only in association with fellows does he become a conscious centre of experience" (1948, 207). Participative decision making is also a necessary condition for development. Like communication, participation requires self-reflection, clarity of thought, imagination, and a sensitivity toward others, greatly enlarging the experience of the participant. Perhaps more importantly, participation develops an awareness of the common interests that underpin community life. With such an awareness, experience is not limited to individual wishes and desires but extends to the community. With this extension, experience is reconstructed to encompass community concerns, enlarging and morally enlightening individual conscious experience. As Dewey suggests, "popular government is educative as other modes of poltical regulation are not. It forces a recognition that there are common interests" (1927, 207). Participation encompasses the developmental features of communication but extends them into the broader arena of political life, thereby increasing their educative power. As Dewey observes, "full education comes only when there is a responsible share on the part of each person, in proportion to capacity, in shaping the aims and policies of the social groups to which he belongs" (1948, 209).

Therefore, according to Dewey, a social arrangement that is conducive to human development provides (1) exposure to a diversity of interests and forms of association; (2) extensive opportunities for communication; and (3) the opportunity to participate in decisions. This type of social arrangement consititues a "democratic community." "Regarded as an idea, democracy is not an alternative to other principles of associated life. It is the idea of community life itself....Democracy is a name for a life of free and enriching community" (1927, 148, 184). Thus, democracy for Dewey is much more than a governmental structure; it is a way of life that is extensively varied, communicative, and participatory. Being a way of life, democracy has an implicit value structure, a value structure that is founded upon the developmental ideal. As Dewey suggests:

All social institutions have a meaning, a purpose. That purpose is to set free and to develop the capacity of human individuals without respect to race, sex, class or economic status. And this is all one with saying that the test of their value is the extent to which they educate every individual into the full stature of his possibility. Democracy has many meanings, but if it has a moral meaning, it is found in resolving that the supreme test of all political institutions and industrial arrangements shall be the contribution they make to the all-around growth of every member of society (1948, 186).

A communicative and participatory social arrangement is democratic in a moral sense, for it provides an equal opportunity for each individual's full potential to unfold. Therefore, for Dewey, democracy and education are virtually indistinguishable. Their conceptual intimacy shaped his vision of the school and its administrative structure.

In *Democracy and Education,* Dewey envisions the school as a democratic community. The school, whose specific purpose is development, must above all other social institutions provide extensive communicative and participatory experiences; it must in its very constitution be democratic.

One dimension of the democratic character of the school is its administrative structure, in particular its policymaking processes. Dewey argues that "the democratic principle requires that every teacher should have some regular and organic way in which he can, directly or through representatives democratically chosen, participate in the formation of the controlling aims, methods and materials of the school of which he is a part" (1946, 63). Dewey argues that if teachers are not allowed to participate in the formation of the educational plan, their skill and sense of responsibility as teachers will be undermined. "The delicate and difficult task of developing character and good judgment in the young needs every stimulus and inspiration possible. It is impossible that the work should not be better done when teachers have that understanding of what they are doing that comes from having shared in forming its guiding ideas" (1946, 65). Dewey argues that if teachers who are directly responsible for the education of the young are not allowed to participate in the policy-formation process, a significant degree of their experience is left uncommunicated. The individual teacher is not developed through the communicative act, and the teacher's experience is not informed by an extensive and diverse range of experience (i.e., the collective experience of the teaching force). The teacher's professional development is correspondingly stunted, and in turn the educational environment that the teacher constructs is equally diminished. Dewey argues that "the absence of democratic methods is the greatest single cause of educational waste" (1946, 65).

Thus, for Dewey, if we are committed to human development as a moral end, then we must be committed to "democracy." We must design our social institutions, including schools, so that they are extensively varied, communicative, and participatory. Social institutions must be arranged so an extensive, freely flowing interaction and communication occur among members and each member participates directly and has equal decision-making power in the policymaking processes of the institution. Although Dewey does not stipulate design specifications for a participative policy process, he clearly invokes the principle of participation as the means to the developmental end. His conception is important, for he is the only theorist among the five discussed in this chapter who specifically connected the developmental conception of democracy to school governance.

Mohandes K. Gandhi

It has often been said of Gandhi that he was a saint in the guise of a politician. There is a semblance of truth in this perception, for Gandhi believed that there was an intimate relationship between politics and spiritual development. In fact, he conceived of politics as a spiritual technique. "My national service is part of my training for freeing my soul from the bondage of flesh. . . .Thus it will be seen that for me there are no politics devoid of religion. They subserve religion. Politics bereft of religion are a death-trap because they kill the soul" (cited in Iyer 1986, 18–19). This developmental conception of politics was not confined to a few, but extended to all individuals: "The whole scheme for the liberation of India is. . .a plan of self purification" (cited in Iyer 1986, 49). In other words, "the purest plan for securing *swaraj* [self-rule] is not to attain a position of isolation but one of full self-realization and self-expression for the benefit of all" (cited in Iyer 1986, 50). Development was Gandhi's guiding political value. "The real question [regarding politics] is how to bring about man's highest intellectual, economic, political, and moral development" (1966, 42). "The end to be sought is human happiness combined with full mental and moral growth" (Gandhi 1962, 34). Like the developmentalists before him, Gandhi maintains that the developmental ideal is the primary standard upon which the value of social institutions should be judged. "I remain loyal to an institution so long as that institution conduces to my growth, to the growth of the nation. Immediately I find that the institution, instead of conducing to growth, impedes it, I hold it my bound duty to be disloyal to it" (Gandhi cited in Fischer 1963, 217). In turn, swaraj was Gandhi's fundamental political principle, for he viewed self-determination as a necessary condition for human development. "If *Swaraj* was not meant to civilize us, and to purify and stabilize our civilization, it would be worth nothing" (1962, 5).

For Gandhi, human development, like life itself, was holistic. Development was "an all-round drawing out of the best in child and man—body, mind, and spirit" (1962, 42). Development thus concerns the actualization of the potential of the whole person. Although Gandhi believed vehemently in individual freedom, he viewed the individual as "a social being" (Fischer 1963, 193). For Gandhi, as was the case for Marx and Dewey, individuality was in part socially constructed. Like the developmentalists before him, Gandhi perceived an intimate relationship between institutional authority and human character.

Gandhi firmly believed that the unfolding of the best in each individual was contingent upon the existence of "non-violent" social institutions. "Non-violence is the law of our species, as violence is the law of the brute. The spirit lies dormant in the brute and he knows no law but that of physical might. The dignity of man requires obedience to a higher law" (Gandhi, cited in Chatterjee 1984, 3). Violence, however, is not confined to physical force. In fact, more potent forms of violence are exploitation and coercion (Chatterjee 1984, 3), which are violent because they rob the individual of freedom to experiment, to experience, and to decide upon a course of action. Development for Gandhi was an active, experimental process. He conceived education, for example, in terms of experimentation (Gandhi 1966). This process necessarily involves the testing of ideas through action and remodification of those ideas in light of direct experience. Gandhi perceived his life as an "experiment with truth" (Iyer 1986, 42). If the individual is exploited and coerced, however, then he or she is denied the freedom to conduct experiments and is thus cut off from genuine development. As Gandhi suggests, "the right to err, which means the freedom to try experiments is the universal condition of all progress" (cited in Iyer 1983, 354).

In terms of the authority structures of institutions, Gandhi viewed the centralization of power as the essence of violence, for centralization necessarily implies coercion, the enforcement of decisions upon others (Chatterjee 1984, 71; Gandhi 1962, 39). He maintains that "centralization as a system is inconsistent with a non-violent structure of society" (1962, 34). Thus Gandhi mused, "I look upon an increase in the power of the State with the greatest fear, because it does the greatest harm to mankind by destroying individuality which lies at the root of all progress" (cited in Chatterjee 1984, 20). Gandhi went as far as to suggest that even if the decision makers in a centralized system are elected by the people, violence would still be perpetuated. He argued that representative democracy is psuedo democracy, for it is ultimately based upon coercion rather than self-rule. "Democracy in the West is, in my opinion, only so-called. . .Western Democracy as it functions today [1939], is diluted Nazism or Fascism" (Gandhi, cited in Chatterjee 1984, 71). Therefore, Gandhi concludes that "democracy cannot be worked by twenty men sitting at the center. It has to be worked from below by the people of every village" (cited in Bhardwaj 1980, 11).

Gandhi maintains that the "essence of non-violence is decentralization" (cited in Chatterjee 1984, 71). Nonviolence requires individual self-rule (swaraj); a completely nonviolent administrative structure would consist of individuals free to govern themselves, to decide their own course of action. Thus Gandhi concludes that "a society organized and run on the basis of complete non-violence would be purest anarchy" (cited in Iyer 1983, 187). However, "enlightened anarchy" for Gandhi was an ideal to be strived for; it was improbable that a pure anarchist system could exist, although, he believed that "village swaraj" was imminently possible (Gandhi, 1962).

Village swaraj constitutes a decentralized, participative system of political organization, wherein each local village is democratically self-governing (Gandhi 1962; Sharma 1987). In this system the total adult population of each village, including women, constitutes the legislative assembly of the village. From this assembly five individuals are unanimously elected as delegates, referred to as the village *"Panchayat."* As delegates, these individuals would directly execute the will of the people derived from a process of consensual decision making conducted in the village assembly. As was the case in Marx's communal system, delegates are revocable.

Each village is connected to a federation of village Panchayats. Each village Panchayat selects a delegate to sit on a district Panchayat, each district sends a delegate to the state Panchayat, and each state sends a delegate to the national Panchayat. Intergovernmental relations between the village and other higher

Panchayats are defined in terms of assistance, information, and coordination. The important decisions regarding the fundamental issues of village life (e.g., education, agriculture, industry, trade and commerce, sanitation, and finance and taxation) are decided on the village level. Sovereignty is thus located in the village, the higher units reflecting that sovereignty (Gandhi 1962; Sharma 1987). Gandhi (1962) described this political arrangement in terms of ascending circles rather than a pyramid structure, wherein the hub was the individual as a sovereign member of a village.

A fundamental notion in Gandhi's political system is consensual decision making. He held that majority rule was fundamentally coercive, for the destiny of the minority is dictated by the majority. Swaraj cannot be identified with majority rule (Iyer 1983, 537). To be truly identified with self-rule and thus democratically nonviolent, consensus has to be reached among all parties. For example, this was the fundamental criterion for India's independence. Gandhi maintained that the only acceptable way for India to gain independence was for the British government to freely consent to leave, to "quit India," which it did in 1947.

Conflicts of interest exist in every social group and must be resolved before consensus can be reached. Under majority rule, conflicts are "resolved" through coercive means; a vote is taken and the issue is resolved in favor of the majority. However, this procedure is coercive relative to the minority, which is forced to abide by a decision to which it is opposed. Violence is done to the minority. Perhaps Gandhi's most brilliant insight is that partial truth exists on both sides of a conflict. Consensus can be reached by (1) examining the principles of both sides to discern the truth of each, which deserves to be a part of the resolution; (2) discerning any points of agreement in truths existing on each side; and (3) constructing alternatives consistent with shared truths. Thus, by discerning the truth of each side, an alternative can be proposed that can be agreed upon by each (See Chapter 3).

Gandhi felt that village swaraj as outlined previously was "true democracy realized" (1962, 71). Under such a regime "we would regard the humblest and lowest Indian as being equally the ruler of India" (1962, 71). This system would provide every adult with the opportunity to participate in the decision-making processes of his or her society. This society would be organized in such a way that the individual would be provided with the maximum freedom and opportunity to undergo the fullest intellectual, moral, and spiritual development possible.

For Gandhi, as is the case for all the theorists discussed in this chapter development is the moral substance of democracy, for it is through democratic participation that optimal human development is achieved. The intellectual, moral, and spiritual development of the individual is the ultimate end of government. In terms of the decision-making process itself, like Marx's communal model, the village Panchayat system is a delegatory one wherein the people select delegates who directly represent their preferences rather than act with independent judgment. In addition, consensus, achieved through nonviolent negotiation, is the standard of legitimacy for each decision. Thus, Gandhi contributes the principle of nonviolence as well as delegation, a compound structure and consensus.

Synthesis

Is it possible to construct a general conception of developmental democracy based upon the political thought of these theorists? In their own way each is arguing that human "development" should be the guiding value in designing systems of governance, that development is contingent upon political "participation," among other principles, and that development is the moral substance of democracy. All, except Dewey, then derive design specifications consistent with their conception of development and participation. However, given their stipulative use of language and their different overarching political perspectives, a general conception of developmental democracy based on their thought would necessarily have to be more a "constellation" or cluster of similar ideas that bear a "family resemblance" rather than a uniform set of ideas derived from a core set of axioms.[12]

The Value of Development

The value of development has two dimensions: substance and process. Concerning substance, all five theorists emphasize the all-around growth of the individual, or what Gandhi refers to as "drawing out the best" in the individual. For Gandhi, this is spiritual development, for the very "spirit" of the individual is being actualized (1962, 42). For Dewey, democracy and education as institutions are defined in terms of "the contribution they make to the all-around growth of every member of society" (1948, 186). This notion of all-around growth is also implicit in Mill's developmental thinking, as exemplified in the epigraph to *On Liberty:* "The grand, leading principle...the absolute and essential importance of human development in its richest diversity." It can also be argued that both

Marx and Rousseau adher to this conception, even though they conceive development unidimensionally, for creativity and virtue are for each theorist the essence of humanity, and thus development concerns the growth of the whole individual. Although concerned with all-around growth, the development of individual capacities are also emphasized.

First, the five theorists surveyed herein are all concerned with the moral development of the individual. In each case the moral growth of the individual is significantly linked to an apprehension of common interests, which is the foundation of community. Moral development is thus premised upon knowing the public interest and acting to preserve community life. Thus, moral development is by definition intimately connected to community. Consequently, a facet of the developmental conception is the notion of moral growth grounded in community life. This notion is exemplified in Rousseau's "virtuous citizen," Mill's rejection of enlightened despotism on moral grounds, Marx's communal ethic, Dewey's conception of democracy as community life, and Gandhi's notion of politics as morally purifying.

In addition, Mill, Marx, Dewey, and Gandhi are also conerned with the intellectual development of the individual. In general, they conceive of intellectual development as involving the growth of one's capacity to discriminate, judge, reflect, reason, create, and communicate. Thus, intellectual development is broadly conceived as encompassing the growth of the full range of one's mental capacities. Therefore, moral and intellectual development are important dimensions of an all-around growth of the individual.

Concerning the process of development, there is common agreement among the theorists that the process is active rather than passive. In each case, whether development is conceived as being moral, intellectual, spiritual, creative, or the all-around growth of the individual, it requires active engagement. Hence such principles as participation, association, communication, and nonviolence are posited, for they all entail dynamic social interaction.

More specifically, for all the theorists the process of human development is one of drawing out and shaping innate potentialities through social interaction. For Marx, human beings are innately creative; for Dewey, they are active, curious, and social; for Gandhi, human beings are inherently free and spiritual; for Rousseau, the individual possesses innate capacities that develop naturally in addition to being shaped by social interaction; for Mill, the individual possesses innate faculties of mind. In all of these cases the individual is not conceived as entering the world as a blank slate. Rather, the individual possesses innate potentialities actualized and shaped through social interaction.

From this constellation of conceptions of the substance and process of development a general notion of "development" can be derived. They form a conception of human development as the actualization and formation of the individual's potential through active engagement with the social environment.

Principles

All five theorists view participation in the decision-making processes of social institutions as a necessary condition for optimal human development. However, participation is a complex, multidimensional idea that assumes different degrees and formats. In addition, participation can only be conceived in relation to the actual content or type of decision. First, I will entertain decisional content, and move then to a consideration of the degree and format of participation. Although somewhat of a digresssion, this discussion will bring to light the complexity of participation.

We can begin discerning decisional content with the basic notion of human association as outlined by the theorists. For them, the defining characteristic of human association is the existence of common interests, those collectively shared interests that unify the social group. If there exists genuine community defined by common interests, then policies consistent with these interests will need to be reflected upon and deliberated collectively. These decisions are essentially legislative rather than executive in nature in that they concern broad policy considerations. Therefore, decisional content is conceived in terms of a separation between legislative and executive decisions, legislative decisions concerning broad policy reflecting the public interest whereas executive decisions concern the implementation of those broad policies.

The legislative decision-making process entails at least three distinguishable stages: (1) agenda-setting; (2) alternative formation; and (3) alternative selection (Dahl 1985; Kingdon 1984). The agenda-setting stage consists of the identification and specification of issues that require consideration. The alternative formation stage involves the specification of alternatives relative to each issue on the agenda. The selection stage consists of choice among a variety of alternatives relative to each issue. In this final state, a decision is made. These three stages are basic to any decision-making process. Consequently, the degree and format of participation can be conceived in relation to legislation as it evolves in each stage.

The degree of participation refers to the distribution of decision-making power, that is, the amount of power alloted to each person (Dachler and Wilpert 1978). On the one hand, every person party to a decision may be granted equal decision-making power. This is "full participation." On the other hand, certain persons may be given the opportunity to express their preferences and have those preferences taken into consideration in the decision-making process while ultimate decision-making power is retained by a superior or the votes of particular individuals may be given more weight. This is "partial participation."[13] Rousseau, Dewey, Marx, and Gandhi advocate full participation; by advocating a voting system weighted in favor of competence, however, Mill provides only partial participation to the majority. The developmental ideal mandates full participation.

The format of participation refers to the structural nature of participation (Conway 1984). Structure can be conceived in terms of two characteristics: formality and directness. On the one hand, participation may be structured formally in the sense that decision-making forums are preestablished (e.g., school council meetings). On the other hand, participation may be informal in the sense that it occurs outside of a preestablished form (e.g., a telephone inquiry). Given that the concern of constitutional choice is the establishment of formal decision-making structures, all considerations concerning the format of participation entertained here are formal in nature.

Within a formal structure, however, participation can be either direct or indirect. It is direct whenever participants are given the opportunity to participate in actual decision making. It is indirect when participation is limited to representatives (Conway 1984; Dachler and Wilpert 1978; Locke and Schweiger 1979). The notions of delegation and representation put forth by Mill, Gandhi, and Marx are examples of indirect participation. Rousseau rejects all notions of indirect participation, exclusively advocating direct participatory democracy. In general, the developmental ideal calls for full and direct participation.

Competing value claims, however, may delimit the degree and format of participation. From the perspective of the developmental tradition, participation is conceived as a means to development rather than as an end. If participation is conceived as a means, it is contingent and being contingent it can not only be constrained but denied. However, all public values exist in comparative tension with each other, so even as ends they can be constrained or denied (Guthrie 1980; Rein 1976). Although somewhat of a digression, it is important here to discuss claims against full and direct participation rendered by competing values. The values of economic liberty, efficiency, competence, and public interest will be discussed as potentially in conflict with development and thereby delimiting to full and direct participation. It will be argued that among these values the value of public interest is the only value that can legitimately delimit participation.

First, an inherent tension exists in classical liberalism between the value of liberty (construed primarily as economic) and the value of political equality, the claim of full and direct participation (Dahl 1985; Macpherson 1966). The classical liberal conception of these values has its origin in Lockean political theory. On the one hand, Locke (1947) argues that the individual possesses a natural right to pursue economic activity, defined in terms of the mixture of labor and nature that yields property, without coercive interference from the state or other individuals and to control the property generated from that activity. On the other hand, political equality is based upon consent. In Locke's view, a civil government is legitimate only insofar as it is derived from the consent of the governed. However, political equality is conceived here as an accountability mechanism designed to protect property owners from the coercive interference of the state (Held 1987; Macpherson 1966, 1977). That is, participation is viewed as a means to protect economic liberty. From this perspective, consent is required of only property owners, thereby justifying exclusion of significant groups from participation.

However, by justifying the participation of property-owners on the basis of consent, the door is open to a universal claim for political equality (Macpherson 1966). This claim is based not on property rights, however, but on developmental grounds. The theorists surveyed above conceived self-determination (full and direct participation) in terms of developmental liberty rather than economic liberty. When the requirement of consent is viewed from this perspective, every person has a human right to full and direct participation. Here the inherent tension between liberty and equality dissolves. Liberty and equality are no longer distinct and conflictual, but they become virtually indistinguishable (Macpherson 1973).

Second, as discussed in chapter 1 the value of efficiency is one of the most significant justifications for the delimitation of participation in governance. Efficiency is based upon the utilitarian principle of maximizing collective benefits. The calculus of efficiency is thus set in terms of cost-benefit analysis. It is maintained that centralized decision-making structures cut costs by controlling the conception of production which eliminates the waste of worker discretion, thereby increasing net benefit. However, it has become apparent that centralized systems are not efficient in this sense: (1) they entail enormous enforcement costs (Bowles and Gintis 1986); (2) they are inherently rigid, impeding innovation (Reich 1983); and (3) by restricting self-determination they undermine the development of human creativity. From this perspective, efficiency may not only be compatible with participative structures, it may demand them (Reich 1983). As Dewey pointed out, undemocratic systems of governance are the source of inefficiency.[14]

Third, there is a potential conflict between the claim for full and direct participation on developmental grounds and the claim for expert control on the grounds of competence. Historically, this conflict has been at the heart of the struggle for democracy. Plato (1979), for example, argues against democracy on the grounds that (1) the general population is only capable of "opinion"; (2) government, if it is to be "just," requires policy based upon "knowledge"; (3) only a few individuals, philosophers, are capable of attaining knowledge; and therefore, (4) governmental policy should be formulated by an elite group of philosopher-kings. The result of this argument is an "aristocratic" system of government wherein the best-qualified rule. It is a system of guardianship premised on competence. Corporate liberalism, which provided the justification for the centralization of governance in the Progressive Era, shifts the claim to participation from property rights to competence in that scientific expertise became the criterion for decision-making power (Mill also favors competence). From this perspective, competence takes precedence over political equality.

From a developmental perspective, political equality does not have to be subordinate to competence. Rather, they may be complementary. This complementarity is based upon the distinction between the authoritative and the democratic use of expertise. The distinction is fundamentally a difference between the exclusive control of decision making by experts and the consulting of experts in a process of democratic deliberation. Just as a jury draws on expert testimony in order to reach a sound decision, a community may want to draw on expert knowledge. While it is informed by expert knowledge, the final decision remains the prerogative of the people. This is the democratic use of expertise (Dewey 1927). The people, however, may also choose, not only to consult, but also to delegate certain decisions to experts. This is especially true regarding executive decisions related to policy implementation. Therefore, even in a system of government designed to allow maximum participation expert authority has a legitimate place in terms of both democratic consultation and executive discretion.

Fourth, on the basis of the size principle, policymaking bodies must be limited in size to a relatively small number. This size principle caused Mill to advocate representation. However, Rousseau maintains that, given the developmental importance of direct participation, the size principle mandates the decentralization of decision making rather then delimiting participation to an indirect format. However, as Gandhi, Dewey, and Marx maintain, certain issues may concern larger publics than the immediate community; society is inevitably comprised of overlapping publics. As Dewey suggests, a public is a "large body of person's having a common interest in the consequences of social transactions" (1927, 137). Or in Rousseau's terminology, a public is a human association governed by the social contract. Therefore, if according to the size principle decision making is decentralized, the larger publics may not be represented. Thus, it can be argued that a degree of centralization may be legitimate based upon the claim of public interest. This need for centralization would limit participation to an indirect format. Thus, the claim of public interest is potentially delimiting to the format of participation.

Therefore, based upon the considerations of the competing value claims of liberty, efficiency, competence, and public interest that could justify the delimitation of participation, the value of development is resistant to the first three claims, but the value of public interest may partially constrain its participatory mandate. This constraint has significant implications for the structure of the decision-making system discussed in chapter 3.

Besides the general agreement concerning the importance of participation, four other principles are derived from the developmental ideal: communication, association, nonviolence, and community. The principles of communication and association are derived from Mill's notion of liberty of thought, discussion, and association and Dewey's conception of democracy as a free, varied, and communicative form of social life. Gandhi contributes the principle of nonviolence. Optimal human development cannot occur in a manipulative, coercive, abusive environment; development requires nonviolence. As discussed above, all five theorists also posit the existence of a "public interest," which entails the life of the community as a whole. In this case, the common interest is not a collective will existing independently of private will, but is pragmatically grounded in and constructed out of private interest. This recognition implies another principle, that of community. However, as already pointed out, there is an inherent conflict between the principle of participation and the principle of community in large-scale modern societies.[15]

Thus, the constellation of principles consistent with the value of development includes participation, association, communication, nonviolence, and community. As we will see below the conflict between participation and community can be resolved through particular design structures.

Design

Design concerns the nature and structure of the decision-making process. Mill, Marx, and Gandhi all call for a compound structure of decision making in order to accommodate as much participation as possible while being sensitive to the public interest. Rousseau is the only theorist who resists the modern impulse, premised on the size principle, to move to some kind of indirect format. The key to the legitimacy of a compound structure is the nature of representation. Mill conceives representation in terms of a grant of authority, whereas Marx and Gandhi conceive representation in terms of delegation. Delegation attempts to preserve a degree of decentralization in order to accommodate direct participation, while simultaneously attempting to accommodate the public interest. Delegates are not free to exercise independent judgment (i.e., they are not given a grant of authority). Rather, they carry the mandate of the people to the legislative forum, in essence re-presenting the interests of the people. Delegation preserves a high degree of direct participation; for each citizen has the opportunity to participate in significant political deliberation. Hence, a compound structure based upon delegation is the way that Gandhi and Marx resolve the conflict between participation and community (other structures are discussed in chapter 3).

In addition, both Rousseau and Gandhi maintain that the legitimacy of a decision should be judged in terms of consensus. Consensus for Rousseau is a measure of the extent to which the general will (public interest) is known, whereas for Gandhi, a consensual decision is the only one that is nonviolent. In addition, the formation of a consensus involves a considerably greater degree of deliberation than majority rule, which increases the developmental potential of participation (see chapter 3). Mill, on the other hand, in order to prevent majority tyranny advocates a voting system weighted in favor of competence. This system, however, is open to minority tyranny and also undermines full and direct participation for every citizen.

A compound structure premised upon delegation and consensual decision making forms a constellation of design specifications consistent with the principles of participation, association, communication, nonviolence, and community. A compound structure is simultaneously sensitive to the principle of participation and the principle of community. Delegation is consistent with the principles of participation and communicaton, for delegation requires participation in agenda-setting and alternative formation and free and extensive communication among delegates and constituents. Consensual decision making is fundamentally nonviolent and involves extensive participation and communication.

In summary, a constellation of ideas that forms the developmental conception of democracy emerges from the thought of the five theorists surveyed herein. This constellation includes the value of development, defined as the actualization and formation of the individual's moral, intellectual, spiritual, and creative capacities through dynamic social interaction. It includes the principles of participation, association, communication, community, and nonviolence, and the design features of delegation, a compound structure and consensual decision making. We now turn to the design of school governance based upon this conception.

3

Design

The purpose of this chapter is to articulate design features concerning the restructuring of school governance which are consistent with the developmental conception of democracy outlined in chapter 2. This conception includes the value of development and the principles of participation, association, communication, community, and nonviolence, which incorporate the design features of a compound structure, delegation, and consensual decision making. However, a number of alternative design features consistent with these principles will also be entertained.

Alternative Structures

Isonomy

"Democracy" was originally conceived as rule (*cracy*) by the many (*demos*), or more specifically rule of the common people. However, the Greek polis was conceived by its participants not as rule of one group over another, whether monarchy, aristocracy, or democracy, but rather as self-governance, or as no-rule in the sense that there was no distinction between ruler and ruled. The polis was an *isonomy* rather than a democracy (Arendt 1962). This is precisely the position taken by Rousseau, who argues that once the division between ruler and ruled occurs the body politic dissolves. From this perspective, to be ruled over, even by a representative, is violent, thereby undermining the developmental potential of the polis. Self-governance or developmental liberty requires the establishment of public forums wherein each participant fully and directly participates in the decision-making process and no distinction exists between ruler and ruled. From this perspective, full and direct participation for every individual is the only legitimate form of participation. Given the size principle, self-governance in turn requires the decentralization of decision making. In Rousseau's view this meant limiting the body politic to small city-states.

The implications for the structure of school governance are profound. From this perspective, the school itself would have to become an independent polis, wherein its policies were deliberated and decided in a politically equal forum. In this sense the school would be self-governing, constituting an independent, sovereign body. The larger society would be comprised of any number of free-floating, independent schools. This is not to suggest that this structure would be exclusively a free market in which the choice of a school outside of one's immediate community would be available, but where schools would exclusively serve the local community and be governed by it.

This structure views all forms of regulation external to the sovereignty of the school as illegitimate. However, implicit in this structure and its rejection of external regulation and control is the view that the individual school is a self-contained public. Given that each school has an identifiable common interest, it constitutes a public and thus has a legitimate claim to sovereignty. In our current interdependent society, however, the school coexists within larger publics, and thus it can be argued that, based upon the principle of community, a claim of external sovereignty is also legitimate. Isonomy is thus inconsistent with the principle of community in large-scale modern societies.

Free Market Structure

A free market structure is an attempt to provide an individual with the power to make public choices. In essence, it is an attempt to provide the individual with self-determination while simultaneously providing the school with autonomy. The argument is that self-determination is best, or perhaps can only be, ensured through a free market system wherein choice or decision is left to the individual consumer. From this perspective free market structures and democracy are inseparable (Friedman 1962). A free market system of schooling in the form of voucher systems or tax credits, which is a significant part of the current school restructuring movement (chapter 4), would allow parents and students to choose the school the students would attend. This is potentially a significant format of direct participation. In addition, it is similar in some ways to isonomy in the sense that the school would be completely autonomous, for a true free market would be unregulated. However, this structure has significant problems.

First, even in the case of a completely free market choice, the participant is restricted to the selection of alternatives already formed; he or she has no input into the alternatives to be selected (Herman 1992). Thus, participation is only partial; there is choice but no sovereignty. If, however, the consumer could not only choose the school but also play an equal part in its governance, then isonomy would be achieved.

Second, and closely associated to the first objection, is that choice renders public decisions into private choices. Instead of asking, for example, "What is a good system of public education for *our* children?" a free market structure transforms the question into, "What kind of school do I want for *my* children?" (Barber 1984, 296, emphasis in the original). Community and the common interest are lost in this transformation. This is clearly inconsistent with the principle of community, but it is also inconsistent with the principle of participation in that the developmental dimension of participation is lost when there is no collective deliberation concerning the public interest. Thus, a free market structure disregards both participation and community.[1]

To solve these problems, while preserving its possible benefits, the free market approach could be combined with isonomy. This structure would allow each individual to choose a school and significantly participate in its governance. The problem of the wider public interest remains, however, and thus the combination still violates the principle of community.

Compound Structure

One alternative for resolving the conflict between the developmental claim for direct participation and the necessity of collective deliberation is an integrated compound structure with multiple, overlapping decision-making assemblies wherein sovereignty is shared (chapter 2).

In keeping with isonomy, within a given school an agenda can be formed, and a school assembly can specify alternatives premised on the full and direct participation of parents, teachers, citizens, administrators, and, if appropriate, students. When an issue concerns the school alone, a decision can be deliberated and rendered. However, when decisions are identified that not only affect an individual school but also have consequences for larger publics such as the district, these decisions will need to be collectively deliberated and decided upon by all members of the district, region, state, and/or nation. Such deliberation could only take place in more centralized assemblies.

Consequently, although initial agenda-setting and alternative selection can and should take place in individual school assemblies, thereby preserving a degree of direct participation, selection, the third stage in the decision-making process, may be reserved for more centralized assemblies.

Given the size principle, however, participation in the more centralized assemblies will be limited to an indirect format. However, as discussed in chapter 2, the question of representation then becomes extremely important. As Marx and Gandhi suggest, "republicanism" is a weak form of democracy, for in a representative system the election of representatives is inherently a grant of authority from the people to a select few (see also Pateman 1975). This grant of authority for all practical purposes constitutes a transfer of sovereignty. This conclusion calls the nature of representation in compound republics into question.

When the framers of the U.S. Constitution met in Philadelphia in 1787 they agreed that the Articles of Confederation were inadequate, particularly concerning the weakness of the national government (Dahl 1967). The question was, How strong should the national government be? The state Federalists were in favor of a relatively weak national government and thus supported a concept of federalism wherein sovereignty would be primarily located on the state level. On the other hand, the national Federalists believed in an equal compound republic.

In the view of the national Federalists the Articles of Confederation had two fundamental flaws: the national government had neither sovereignty over nor did it represent individuals (Dahl 1967). On the one hand, for a national government to have validity it had to possess formal authority over individuals. The national Federalists understood that the granting of authority to one government over another is a logical contradication. A government can only have legal authority over individuals, not other governments (Ostrom 1985), hence the notion of a federal system of government containing a compound of polities with shared sovereignty. On the other hand, the requirement of power over individuals necessitates, in democratic systems, the consent of the individual. If the national government has power over individuals, then under the tenets of democracy those individuals must be repesented directly. This conception of federalism is consistent with the "national theory" of American federalism, wherein it is held that a single sovereign power, the people, created both the federal and state governments and delegated to each a certain limited authority (Beer 1978).

However, if the people are the creators of government and that government is created not as a Hobbesian leviathan wherein the people—upon entering the political contract—grant absolute authority to the government but as representative of the people, then representation conceived as a grant of authority is illegimate. A grant of authority transfers sovereignty from the constituents to the representative, thereby undermining democratic consent. Rather, representation must be conceived not as a grant of authority, but as the re-presentation in governmental forums of the will of the people. Therefore, if we adhere to the national theory of compound republics, rather than the compact theory which holds that the states created the national government, representation must be conceived as delegation or some other form of representation which does not transfer soveriegnty. In principle, delegation does not entail a grant of decision-making authority to the representative. Rather, the delegate delivers constitutents decisions to a more central assembly. The constituency has set the agenda, formulated the alternatives, and has sent the delegate to the assembly. The delegate is charged with arguing for the constituents' mandate and, in this sense, is truly representative.

It can be argued, however, that the delegate will be constrained by this mandate and not be able to negotiate, thus undermining the grounds for deliberation. Consequently, the delegate, while representing the constituents' mandate, must be given freedom to negotiate and possibly compromise. Negotiation, however, should be shaped by significant input from constituents, allowing them to be party to the negotiation. If genuine representation is to exist without undermining negotiation, extensive lines of communication among constitutents and delegates must be maintained. Delegation so designed can enable free, extensive communication between representatives and constituents, which, while being structured in terms of an indirect format, preserves many of the developmental benefits of direct participation.

This structure is simultaneously decentralized and centralized in the sense that a functional relationship exists between extensive participative decentralization and more centralized decision-making bodies (Coombs 1987). It is a structure premised upon shared sovereignty, which is simultaneously participatory and sensitive to the public interest. It is also consistent with the principle of association, for it provides the opportunity for interaction with a varied number of different social groups. It is consistent with the principle of communication, for a delegatory system demands a free and extensive flow of communication between delegates and constituents. And it is consistent with the principle of community, for it allows for common interests to be deliberated collectively and decided upon by all concerned. A compound structure thus holds the possibility of resolving the conflict between participation and community. There are, however, other alternatives.

Deliberative Opinion Polls

In *Democracy and Deliberation,* James Fishkin (1991) posits the idea of "deliberative opinion polls," that is, polling a statistically representative sample of the population who are provided an opportunity to engage in extensive political deliberation. They thereby reflect what the general population would think if given the same deliberative opportunity. An ordinary opinion poll reflects what the citizenry thinks without significant opportunities, in many cases, for deliberation concerning the polling issue. Preferences shaped by the mass media are merely "bounced back. . .without sufficient critical scrutiny and without sufficient information and examination to represent any meaningful popular control" (Fishkin 1992, 19). In contrast, a deliberative opinion poll is designed to model "what the electorate *would* think if, hypothetically, it could be immersed in intensive deliberative processes. . .telling us. . .what the entire mass public would think about some policy issues or some candidates if it could be given an opportunity for extensive reflection and access to information" (81). The deliberative opinion poll provides a public forum wherein a "representative microcosm of the mass public can become deliberative" (84).

Fishkin derives the deliberative opinion poll from the ancient Athenian jury. The Athenian jury, comprised of approximately five hundred citizens selected by lot, was charged with "trying" the legislative decisions of the Athenian assembly. The jury was empowered to "explicitly reconsider and overturn the decisions of the Assembly" (88).[2] The power of the jury in turn impelled the assembly to engage in thoughtful deliberation, for they knew their decisions would be reconsidered and possibly sanctioned. Fishkin maintains that these juries "were miniature, statistically representative versions of the entire citizenry who were given wide discretion in making political judgments for the polity" (88). Given the size and complexity of modern society, Fishkin envisions the deliberative opinion poll as a modern version of the Athenian jury.

The deliberative opinion poll based upon the Athenian jury is an alternative structure for solving the conflict between participation and community, for it simultaneously provides extensive deliberative, participatory opportunities as well as a way to consider the common interest. If we apply the deliberative poll to school governance, a compound structure may not be needed. One can envision a structure with a centralized decision-making body informed by periodic deliberative opinion polls that would provide an agenda, alternatives, and preferences. Thus, the state legislature could assume its constitutional authority over educational policy while being significantly determined by a representative sample of the deliberations of its constituency. The problem with this structure, however, is that although it is sensitive to community, it only ensures the participation of a representative sample of the population, in principle a small number. Thus, it is inconsistent with the principle of participation.

To remedy the problem, while preserving the potential of this idea, the notion of political juries and/or a deliberative opinion poll could be combined with a compound structure, becoming in essence a means of representation. Each indivdual school assembly could be polled. The results, in terms of the agenda, alternatives, and preferences of such a poll, which would be deliberative because they would emerge from a participatory assembly, would then inform the decisions of more centralized assemblies. These assemblies could also be subject to periodic oversight by jury, thereby combining the power of both deliberative polls and juries. Central decision-making bodies— (for example, the state legislature, school boards of large urban districts, and the educational committees of Congress)—could be subject to oversight ("trial") by juries comprised of individuals selected from local school assemblies. Local school assemblies would retain control of decisions that affect them exclusively and provide deliberative opinions to more centralized assemblies. They could also provide a rotating membership to juries charged with overseeing the decisions of more centralized bodies, thereby directly and indirectly influencing the decisions of these bodies. The combination of deliberative opinion polling and oversight juries with a compound structure possesses a high participatory quality and allows significant collective deliberation concerning the public interest.

In summary, the fundamental issue concerning developmental decision-making structures is the conflict between participation and community. Four alternative structures have been entertained (not by any means an exhaustive list), revealing the complexity of this conflict and providing a set of possible alternatives for resolving it. Isonomy offers full and direct participation but is insensitive to the public interest. A free market structure offers a limited degree of participation (as choice) while also neglecting the public interest. A combination of isonomy and a free market structure would allow significant direct participation, but it would still violate the principle of community. However, a compound structure premised upon delegation, deliberative opinion polling, and/or oversight juries would provide a significant degree of direct participation while being sensitive to the public interest, thereby being consistent with both the principles of participation and community.

Decision Rules

Decision rules govern the formal decision-making process. They specify how decision making should proceed and what defines a legitimate decision. The following decision rules are consistent with the developmental ideal: consensus as opposed to majority rule, the oversight criteria of nonrepression and nondiscrimination, due process, and juridical standards.

Consensual Decision Making

As Benjamin Barber points out, in the public arena conditions exist that "impose a necessity for public action, and thus for reasonable public choice" (1984, 120). These choices are fundamentally "political," for choosing is necessarily done in the face of conflict and in the absence of "independent grounds of judgment" that would provide a basis for resolving conflict by appeal to a priori standards (120–122). Politics becomes the way conflict is resolved and reasonable choices are made in the absence of an independent ground of judgment.

Barber (1984) articulates five modes of politics as conflict resolution: authoritative, juridical, pluralist, unitary, and strong democracy, all of which entail some form of consensual decision making but with important differences.

The first mode, the authoritative, is essentially the elite conception of democracy wherein conflict is resolved through deference to an executive elite who possess the competence or expertise necessary to make public choices. It is the ideal of Platonic guardianship, implicitly suggesting a surrogate independent ground based upon expert knowledge. From the developmental perspective, this method of decision making delimits participation, thereby undermining the developmental potential of democracy.

The second mode of politics, "juridical" democracy, is closely akin to the authoritative elite mode but has a judicial twist. It posits that conflict can be resolved through deference to a "representative judicial elite that, with the guidance of constitutional and preconstituional norms, arbitrates difference and enforces constitutional rights and duties" (1984, 142). In this case conflict is resolved through neutral arbitration. Like the authoritative mode judicial democracy delimits participation on the basis of competence.

An alternative mode, having greater democratic appeal, is what Barber refers to as "pluralist democracy." Pluralism resolves conflict through "bargaining and exchange among free and equal individuals and groups, which pursue their private interests in a market setting governed by the social contract" (1984, 143). This mode is exemplified by public choice models and Dahl's (1956) conception of polyarchy. These notions of politics in turn have their theoretical roots in the Madisonian rejection of majority rule.

Running throughout the history of democratic thought is the notion of majority rule. Dahl provides a succinct articulation of the principle of majority rule. "The principle of majority rule prescribes that in choosing among alternatives, the alternative preferred by the greater number is selected. That is, given two or more alternatives x, y, etc., in order for x to be government policy it is a necessary and sufficient condition that the number who prefer x to any alternative is greater than the number who prefer any single alternative" (1956, 37–38).

Thus the principle of majority rule posits that a decision is binding when a greater number of voters prefers it over another alternative. However, despite its widespread acceptance as a decision rule this principle has a fundamental problem. It ignores differences in the intensity of preferences (Dahl 1956). Perhaps a particular policy is only slightly prefered by a narrow majority and its alternative is strongly preferred by the minority. Under the majority prinicple, the policy the majority prefers would be enacted even though the majority was relatively indifferent to it while the minority intensely preferred it. In this case a significant minority is denied what it intensely prefers by a narrow majority. In a Gandhian sense, "violence" is done to the minority, which is forced to abide by the dictates of an indifferent majority. Thus the majority principle is open to the possibility of tyranny in the form of oppression by a majority over minorities.

This possibility was foreseen by Madison and Hamilton, among others, and led them to frame a "consensual democracy." The separation of powers and a compound structure in their view would demand the concurrence of independent authorities in the policymaking process, thereby balancing diverse interests against each other so no interest could become a dominant and entrenched majority (Benn 1967). In this Madisonian system, the government would only be capable of acting when consensus exists (Kelman 1988).

The balancing mechanism that demands the generation of consensus is solely contained within the machinery of government via the provision of checks and balances. Implict in this argument is the proposition that factions will tyrannize others unless restrained by external checks, and that external checks are best provided by "constitutionally prescribed machinery" of government (Dahl 1956). Dahl observes that Madisonian democracy exaggerates the importance of governmental checks, underestimating the importance of the "inherent social checks and balances existing in a pluralist society" (1956, 22). He argues that without social checks and balances it is doubtful that intragovernmental checks on officals would be enough to prevent tyranny. Social checks and balances arise from the fact that American society is constituted by a plurality of groups and interests. What checks the majority is the social and political reality that policy is determined by the efforts of small but active minorities. According to this pluralist view, in order to be democratic, government agencies must be sensitive to a wide range of interests, so any group significantly affected by a policy will have its preferences taken into consideration. Therefore, rather than being a system where a bargained consensus is generated by virtue of the constitutional machinery of government, democracy is a "polyarchy" where a bargained consensus is generated through the competition of a plurality of minority interests (Dahl 1956).

From the perspective of consensual decision making, however, whether a consensus is generated on the basis of internal governmental arrangements or by virtue of the plurality of social groups, both entail what Fisher and Ury (1983) refer to as "positional" negotiation wherein each party to a decision assumes an adversarial posture. Such negotiation leads to a consensus founded upon animosity. It is premised upon self-interest rejecting the existence of a public interest. As Gandhi and Dewey both suggest, however, the means shapes the end attained. Although conflict can be resolved through bargaining, the seeds of future conflict are sowed in the bargain. The assumption of exclusive self-interest becomes a self-fulfilling prophecy producing continual conflict.

Barber's fourth mode of politics, the "unitary," is also consensual but in a conformist rather than a bargained mode. This mode resolves conflict "through community consensus as defined by the identification of individuals and their interests with a symbolic collectivity and its interests" (1984, 149). Conflict is resolved through conformity. Individual and group interests are sacrificed to the interests of an abstract collective will that lacks pragmatic grounding in particular interests, a position of which Rousseau is wrongly accused (chapter 2). Although a consensus is achieved, it is also coerced. In this case, however, the consensus is not derived from bargaining but through conformity. Its coercion is far more dangerous in that it entails a far greater degree of passivity, of blind acceptance of authority. Although consensual, this mode is even less participatory than any of the three preceding modes. At least in the previous modes some kind engagement, either in the form of the selection of elites or in bargaining, is afforded. From this perspective it can be argued that "consensus" is preferable to majority rule if and only if the means to consensus is itself nonviolent and participatory.

This conclusion leads to Barber's fifth mode of politics, "strong democracy in the participatory mode." Strong democracy resolves conflict through a "participatory process of ongoing, proximate self-legislation and the creation of a political community capable of transforming dependent private individuals into free citizens and partial and private interests into public goods" (1984, 151). This mode of decision making is fundamentally participatory, aiming to transform conflict rather than either "suppressing, tolerating, or ameliorating it" (151). What emerges from this process is what Barber refers to as "creative consensus" rather than a coercive, conformist, or a bargained consensus. He defines creative consensus as "an agreement that arises out of common talk, common decision, and common work...that is premised on citizens' active and perennial participation in the transformation of conflict through the creation of common consciousness and political judgement" (224). Through public deliberation values are "imaginatively reconstructed as public norms" (137).

This process is based upon "principled negotiation." Principled negotiation, as opposed to positional negotiation wherein weaknesses are exploited in the bargaining process to further private interests, looks beyond apparent conflicts of interest to deeper levels of commonality (Fisher and Ury 1983). This is a process of what Gandhi refers to as "satyagraha," literally "grasping truth." From this perspective, truth is relative and therefore conflictual. There is no independent ground on the basis of which a decision can be made with certainty. Thus, each individual brings private interests or relative truth to the policymaking process. The inevitable conflict that this public deliberation entails is then transformed through dialogue. Through dialogue it is possible to recongnize a nascent commonality between one's own truth and that of another person. It is a search for some common ground, some common principle upon which all participants can agree. The agreement becomes a public norm. It becomes an independent ground not in a metaphysical but in a pragmatic sense, a ground forged from public, common deliberation premised on individual interests. In the process the individual participant's private truth (interest) becomes informed by a common, public interest.

From this perspective, creative consensus as a decision rule demands engagement in problem-solving, open and extensive communication, dialogue and debate, exposure to a wide variety of options and perspectives, appreciation of other points of view, and perceiving commonality underneath the surface of conflict. In this way creative consensus as a decision rule has the potential to add a profound richness to the developmental potential of participation in decision-making processes.

However, although consensual decision making is designed to eliminate coercion, participation and consensual decision making do not occur in isolation but are embedded in the larger social structure, which is inherently unequal. This unequal social structure is stratified in terms of class, race, and gender, which are interwoven social constructions that comprise a web of relations within which identity is created. Given the inequality of this social web, individuals undergo differential socialization, which in turn lays the foundation for one group to exert power over others. Power is defined here as the capacity to extract another person's inherent abilities for personal benefit, for example, labor power that is extracted in both the public workplace and within the private home (Macpherson 1973; Pateman 1985). The conception of participation in consensual decision making is premised upon an equality of decision-making authority. The existence of stratification and differential socialization threatens, however, to insert power (as extraction) into the decision-making process, thereby undermining its developmental potential. For example, women—who have been socialized to assume passive, subordinate roles and in many cases have had their power extracted in both public and private life— may enter the decision-making process on unequal footing with males, who have been socialized to be aggressive and dominant. The same is true for men and women from subordinate classes and races. This overarching social inequality is likely to allow one group to subtly dominate the consensual process, turning what seems to be formal equality of authority into an unequal power relation (Heller 1991; Macpherson 1973; Nicholson 1986; Okin 1991; Pagano 1991; Pateman 1970, 1980, 1983a, 1983b, 1984, 1985; Roland-Martin 1985).

Given the existence of power relations based upon stratification and differential socialization, one could argue that a large degree of social equality must be achieved for consensual decision making to be viable. This equalization is premised upon the existence of what Macpherson refers to as "counter-extractive liberty" (1973, 118). In other words, if each participant is going to enter the decision-making process on equal footing, he or she must be immune from the extractive power of others. Self-determination (i.e., developmental participation) is contingent upon such immunity. In liberal democratic societies, negative liberty, defined as freedom from coercive interference entailing a protected zone of privacy (Berlin 1969), is guaranteed by a number of constitutional rights. However, this conception of liberty ignores the fact that extraction is coercive (Macpherson 1973). For example, negative liberty has traditionally guaranteed that male heads of households are not interferred with in their control of family life. Conversely, the other members of the family, the wife and children, are traditionally not guaranteed immunity from control of the father. The extraction of a wife's power for the benefit of a husband is often not considered to be in violation of the wife's negative liberty (Okin 1991). In the case of labor power exchanged in the public marketplace, "unequal access to the means of life and labor inherent in capitalism" forces workers to sell their labor power, which directly interfers with their liberty (Macpherson 1973, 101). When individuals only have labor power to exchange they are easily coerced, their power is easily extracted for the benefit of those who own the means of labor (race and gender are also factors, interwoven with class). As even the classical liberal Jeremy Bentham admitted, "In the highest stage of social prosperity, the great mass of citizens will have no resource except their daily industry, and consequently will be always near indigence" (1931, 127; cited in Macpherson 1973, 99). Thus, in order for equal decision-making authority to exist, counterextractive liberty must be widespread. This would entail the democratization of the workplace and the family as well as other social institutions. Short of this social democratization, what can be done to facilitate political equality in school governance?[3]

As Carole Pateman suggests,"Every form of social life requires a specific form of consciousness or 'social spirit' in its members" (1985, 176). Or from the perspective of Paulo Freire (1970), a particular cultural epoch is based upon certain themes that define the consciousness of people in a particular historical moment. Freire maintains that the fundamental theme, the social spirit, of our time is domination. Domination, manifest in various forms of extractive power relations, prevents the liberation of human potential. In order for genuine democratization to occur, human consciousness must be transformed from domination to liberation. However, "the form of consciousness needed for, and that will be further developed within, the new social order must, it seems, already be in existence or change will not be possible" (Pateman 1985, 176). We are caught in paradox.

Freire offers a way out in terms of dialogue, and this is the key to a developmental consensual process. Freire observes that dialogue is transformative for both the oppressed and the oppressor. Through genuine acts of communication various interpersonal barriers, such as fear, moral exclusivity, prejudice, and domination, can be broken down, so that the inherent differences between individuals can be bridged and used as means to solidarity rather than exploitation. In other words, if genuine dialogue can take place, the consciousness of domination can be transformed. Thus, genuine dialogue, based upon cooperation, humility, solidarity, and concern, the creation of an *I-Thou* relationship, is the foundation of consensual decision making. This process is developmental in the sense that the consciousness that would prevent equality is transformed during it. Therefore, the key to ensuring genuine consensual decision making is to create the conditions within which dialogue can occur. In communicating across class, gender, and racial lines rather than issuing communiques, there is the possibility of an equal consensual process.

For the conditions of dialogue to be created, those individuals who have held positions of power within and outside of a school, for example its administrators, must become transformative leaders (as defined in the introduction). It is these individuals who hold the key to democratization. If they act to empower previously disenfranchised participants, then the barriers of extractive power can be dissolved. Of course, the emergence of transformative leaders is contingent upon a change in consciousness. This change may not be easily forthcoming and may entail a substantial rethinking of leadership education in schools of education (see Foster 1986).

In addition, political education in the form of in-service training must be made available to all participants. Participation itself is the primary form of political education, however this does not negate the need for prior preparation. The opportunity to develop the critical abilities necessary for dialogue must be afforded to all those individuals who, because of their socialization, are ill-equiped for political deliberation. In the face of the lack of transformative leadership, prior preparation may include political organizing efforts by already empowered participants in solidarity with those who have been previously disenfranchised. A reinvigoration of unionism in the Haley tradition, in conjunction with community organization efforts, may be in order.

In addition to creating the conditions for dialogue, one of the fundamental guarantees of political equality is the freedom to dissent (Pateman 1985). The protection of this freedom enables any participant in a consensual system to prevent injustice from being perpetrated. On what grounds would legitmate dissent rest? Amy Gutman (1987) offers at least two criteria: the principles of nonrepression and nondiscrimination.

The principle of nonrepression maintains that any decision that confines deliberation to a narrow range of alternatives is subject to veto. This principle is based upon the view that, as Mill suggests, moral and intellectual development is contingent upon exposure to a wide range of opinions, values, and perspectives. It is through critical, reasoned reflection on such a range that one's mind and moral sense are expanded. In other words, to narrow the range of discussion is to repress the developmental value of that discussion. Thus, any decision that would exclude recognizable points of view is invalid and therefore subject to veto on the grounds of the principle of nonrepression.

The principle of nondiscrimination suggests that if a decision favors the development of one group of students over another, or treats groups differently so some are not given an equal developmental opportunity, that decision is invalid. The value of development explicitly concerns the actualization of the full intellectual and moral potential of every student. In American education a long history of discrimination exists along racial, ethnic, class, disability, and gender lines. Therefore, any decision that discriminates and thereby excludes certain groups or individuals from equal educational experiences is invalid and subject to veto under the principle of nondiscrimination. This principle thus entails equal protection under the law.

In case consensus is manipulated and not objected to on these grounds at the time of decision, a due-process provision is added. In order to ensure equity in educational decisions, any party should have the right to appeal a decision rendered by a decision-making assembly on the grounds of repression or discrimination. This due-process clause provides individuals with the power to exercise these criteria, even after the fact. The threat of due process provides greater assurance that the criteria will be adhered to in the decision making process. In fact, oversight juries, guided by these criteria, would be a powerful form of due process.

Political equality can also be facilitated by particular juridical procedures in the sense of how policies are formulated. Theodore Lowi (1979) argues that due to the lack of clear, precise policy, which details standards and procedures for implementation, public policy is redefined in the process of implementation, in many cases in the interest of narrow corporate interests. This in effect, has shifted the policymaking process from a public debate to a private negotiation between dominant interests and the members of government. Lowi refers to this state of government as "interest-group-liberalism" and argues that it is so ingrained in our political structure that it constitutes a second republic, in essence a movement from federal republicanism to elite democracy.

Lowi's solution is a return to constituationalism in the form of what he calls "juridical democracy."[4] The central characteristic of juridical democracy is "rule of law operating in institutions" (1979, 298). Rule of law incorporates three standards: (1) the articulation of public policy in statutory law; (2) specification of implementation and enforcement procedures within the statute; and (3) statutory language enabling the law to be understood by anyone affected by it (Grady 1984). These juridical standards restrict discretion, thereby reinstating legislative authority.

Precise specification of policy through a process of public deliberation provides a juridical mechanism that ensures that all relevant issues and alternatives are publicly known and debated. The requirement of juridical specification as a decision rule is a safeguard for making the decision-making process open and thereby participative. In addition, it also restricts executive discretion so that legislative power cannot be usurped by those charged with implementation, a common practice under interest group liberalism, which undermines the democratic process.

In summary, if consensual decision making is based upon genuine dialogue, facilitated by transformative leadership and political education and organization, open to dissent on the basis of nonrepression and nondiscrimination fortified by due process, and formulated in terms of juridical standards, the likelihood is greater that political equality will be served in spite of social inequality.

In conclusion, a compound structure premised on delegation, deliberative opinion polling, and/or oversight juries provides a decision-making system that is highly participative while sensitive to the public interest. This structure, coupled with consensual decision making grounded in the provisions of political equality, offers a general framework for a democratic system of school governance premised upon the developmental ideal.

4

School Restructuring

The purpose of this chapter is to analyze the educational reform movement of the 1980s from the perspective of the democratic theory and structure of school governance put forth in the preceding two chapters. This analysis will encompass both the theoretical underpinnings of the reform movement, in particular school-based management, and the forms it has taken in various cities and regions in the United States.

The First Wave of Reform

In 1983, the Reagan adminstration-sponsored report *A Nation at Risk* initiated a wave of reform proposals. The report proclaimed that the nation was at risk due to the erosion of the educational foundations of society, what the Commission on Excellence in Education referred to as "a rising tide of mediocrity" (1983, 5). The commission argued that as a nation we have committed "an act of unthinking, unilateral educational disarmament" (1983, 5), in the process losing sight of the basic purposes of schooling.[1] In an era of rising global political and, more important, economic competition this erosion of educational excellence, the report argues, places the United States at risk of losing its preminent place in the world political and economic order.[2]

The recommendations the commission proposed, designed to stem the tide of educational mediocrity and its concommitant risks, were numerous and covered curriculum, standards, use of time, teaching, leadership, and fiscal issues. The report, however, emphasized refocusing the curriculum on mathematics and science, increasing standards and reliance on test scores, establishing tougher discipline, and lengthening the time students spend in school (Beyer 1985).

Numerous states responded to *A Nation at Risk,* as well as to other reports (Gross and Gross 1985), during legislative sessions in 1983 and 1984 (USDE 1984). The focus of such response was primarily on accountability. In general, it was argued that schools would improve if held accountable for the educational achievement of students. Accountability was defined in relation to standards of excellence. In general, these accountability measures took the form of higher certification standards for teachers, higher graduation standards, and higher visibility of school performance (e.g., school report cards). In many states proposals for increased teacher salaries and merit-pay were also enacted (Hess 1991).

In terms of school governance, by consolidating authority these reforms also increase the bureaucratic nature of schooling (Spring 1988; Swanson 1989). A focus on increasing standards as accountability measures is scientific managment revisted. By controlling what standards are used to evaluate performance, one can control the substance of the performance. In the case of education, by controlling the criteria of evaluation one controls the curricular content and instructional method, motivating what is commonly referred to as teaching to the test. In addition, merit pay proposals also encourage managerial centralization by requiring "objective" indicators of teacher performance, for objective standards are needed in order to determine merit fairly. Implict in such indicaters are detailed specifications of teaching style in terms of managerial prerogative.

The bureaucratic model of school governance is based upon a view of teaching as a routine technology. From an organizational perspective the teaching-learning process demands a control strategy entailing a system of input, behavior, and output controls. However, although housed in a bureaucracy, the system is in fact "loosely coupled" (Weick 1976). The first wave of reform perceives the loosely coupled nature of the school system as the cause of educational mediocrity and consequently is an attempt to tighten bureaucratic control through various accountability measures, even to the extent of a *national* curriculum and testing system.

The tightening of bureaucratic control, especially when emanating from more centralized levels of government such as the states and national commissions, insulates the policymaking process from genuine democratic control, thereby rendering local school politics and participation into what Frederich Wirt has called a "marginal politics" (1977, 186–187). Thus, the first wave of reform represents the antithesis of the imperatives of developmental democracy.

The Second Wave of Reform

In contrast to the first wave, the second wave of reform is embodied in the notion of school restructuring, the idea of comprehensive reform centered in individual schools rather than in higher levels of government (Cistone 1989). School restructuring is not monolithic, however; it has at least three variations, two of which entail some form of school-based managment: school choice, professionalization, and community empowerment (Elmore 1988; Hess 1991).

School Choice

The fundamental premise of the school choice movement (as is the general orientation of school restructuring) is that the hierarchical, bureaucratic nature of school governance undermines the autonomy and professionalization of teachers. However, instead of democratizing decision making, the school choice movement advocates a free-market solution to increase institutional autonomy and professionalization. A deregulated, laissez-faire choice system, like the democratic solution, is not a new idea. It dates at least to Adam Smith, Thomas Paine, and, more recently to Milton Friedman (Coons and Sugarman 1978; Friedman and Friedman 1979; Wells 1991). The most recent rendition is Chubb and Moe's *Politics, Markets, and America's Schools* (1990).

Chubb and Moe maintain that school organization is a highly significant variable affecting high school student achievement (one of four variables, the other three being student ability in the sophomore year, SES of the family, and SES of the student body). In turn, they maintain that the quality of school organization (in terms of academic goals, strong leadership, professional teaching, academic programs, and cooperation) is contingent upon institutional autonomy. Chubb and Moe argue that the bureaucracy that grows out of political control undermines the quality of school organization. The solution is privatization via a laissez-faire choice system designed to foster institutional autonomy and in turn school effectiveness through the impetus of free market-competition.

From a democratic perspective, although providing a correct diagnosis in terms of the debilitating effects of bureaucracy, the proposed solution has four fundamental problems. First, free-market school choice ignores the impact of social inequality (in terms of race and class) on freedom of choice. A substantial body of empirical and historical evidence exists to suggest that inherent differential access to various resources such as information and the basic alienation bred by social inequality significantly restrict freedom of choice. Free markets are social constructions that are indifferent to the needs of the disadvantaged. Thus, without regulation to ensure equity, a free-market solution may lead to even greater inequality of educational opportunity than already exists (Cookson 1991; Howe 1991; Kozol 1991; Wells 1991).

Second, as discussed in chapter 3, the participant in a free-market choice system is reduced to being merely a consumer of preformulated programs. The participant is forced to choose among alternatives that he or she has not played a part in formulating. In this case there is choice but no sovereignty, and without sovereignty there can be no real freedom of choice. The result is a kind of negative consumer liberty rather than a positive, self-determined choice.

Third, a free-market model ignores the principle of community (chapter 3). Choice systems render public decisions, which should be democratically deliberated, into private choices decided in the narrow context of exclusive self-interest. This system breeds private consumers rather than democratic citizens. It leads to an attitude of succession into a secluded private life insensitive to human inequality and want (Barber 1984; Kozol 1991; Reich 1991).

Fourth, Chubb and Moe (1990) have a narrow conception of politics. They argue that political control of schools subjects educational authorities to a variety of pressures from special interests that lead them to excessively bureaucratize schools. Implicit in this conception of politics is a free-market pluralist model wherein a plurality of interests competes for influence. What Chubb and Moe want is a "privatized" rather than a political free market. This notion is premised upon a false distinction between public and private, however. The market, whether economic or educational, is not apolitical. It is fundamentally political in that its social relations are relations of power, for they are competitive in principle. This is evident in terms of the effects of social inequality on the ability to compete in the market. Thus, given that we are dealing with the political economy of schooling as opposed to a pure economic model, the only way to guarantee freedom of choice is to politically empower those involved. In the context of human, that is, political, association, participatory democracy, rather than laissez-fairism, is thus a more viable means of empowerment and hence freedom.

School-Based Management

The other two approaches to school restructuring, professionalization and client empowerment, contain degrees of participatory decision making, generally referred to as school-based management. School-based management has two fundamental theoretical tenets: school-level autonomy and participative decision making (Cistone 1989; David 1989; Lindquist and Mauriel 1989; Pierce 1980). Autonomy entails the delegation of decision-making power, at least in part, from the school board and the central office to the teachers, parents, principal, community members, and students of individual schools. The intention is to decentralize the decision-making process, basing it in the primary educational site—the school. This decentralization and empowerment of the local school necessarily entails participative decision making. The intention of school-based management is the improvement of organizational competence and effectiveness by democratizing school governance. It is proposed that participation is a necessary condition for improving school effectiveness, that autocratic control of the educational process undermines the professional development of teachers and parental involvement in the school, thereby undermining the educational process itself. Therefore, it is argued that school autonomy and participative decision making are necessary for school effectiveness. However, as Hess (1991) suggests, there are fundamental differences among models that advocate participatory decision making as a means to professionalization and those that advocate the democratization of school governance in order to empower the community.

The Professionalization Approach to School-Based Management

The professionalization approach maintains that decision-making power should be located as close as possible to the actual educational event. It is argued that through the centralization of decision making, bureaucratic systems of administration disallow teacher participation, thereby undermining their professional development, an argument echoing Margaret Haley and Ella Flagg Young. This view is premised on a conception of teaching as fluid and complex rather than as a routine activity. From this perpsective, learning styles are diverse and teaching is a creative activity. Being creative, in principle it is based upon an integration of the conception and execution of instructional and curricular strategies, just as art is a manifestation of the artist's mental image. This conception of teaching necessitates an organizational structure that directly involves teachers in the formulation of educational policy. If teaching is a fluid, complex, creative act, then a bureaucratic system of governance that disallows teacher participation in the policy process will undermine professional development, in essence de-skilling them just as workers have been de-skilled through scientific management. From this perspective too much bureaucratic control, not too little, is at the heart of educational mediocrity.

In addition, the study of policy implementation suggests that even in a centralized, top-down system of administration, implementors reshape policy to fit a variety of situations and needs (Lipsky 1980; Peters 1984; Yates 1977). From this perspective, policy emerges from the bottom rather than being dictated from above (Mintzberg 1987). There is also a significant evolutionary character to emergent policy, in that policies evolve and change over time; however, this evolution is contingent upon the organization's capacity for learning (Elmore 1978; Majone and Wildavsky 1984).

The emergent, evolutionary perspective is especially relevant for public schools, which have been appropriately described as "loosely coupled" systems (Weick 1976). The imposition of a centralized, bureaucratic system of governance on a loosely coupled system significantly impedes the emergent, evolutionary nature of policy formation. Centralization undermines organizational learning, which, in turn, undermines the school's ability to respond to changing social conditions (Bowles and Gintis 1986; Reich 1983). Over time, the reduced capacity of the school to respond to change erodes the educational quality of the school (Dewey 1937; Grant 1985).

An excellent example of the professionalizaton approach is the school-based management plan being implemented in Santa Fe, New Mexico. Its primary aim is to provide a governance system that affords greater teacher participation in school decision making in order to facilitate professional development.

The school-based management reforms in Santa Fe originated in the efforts of the school district's superintendent, Edward Ortiz. Oritz apparently initiated and implemented the reform without any significant pressure from the community or the teachers (Carnoy and MacDonell 1990).[4] In order to gain legitimacy and important technical assistance, Oritz sought and won a grant for school restructuring from the Matsushita Foundation. This restructuring effort was named the Schools Improvement Program. At its heart is school-based management designed to empower teachers, as is indicated in the original document outlining the Schools Improvement Program:

Teachers have been empowered to envision the kind of school they would like to create. In attempting to reach that vision, through information from consultants, planning time, observations of programs in other schools, and various other assistance and with advice and collegial support from the principal of the school, they can submit an Assistance Request Form to the Executive Committee....Unfortunately, teachers may create schools which are fundamentally different from their current schools. These changes may require the approval of the school board before being implemented and the involvement of parents for successful implementation. Regardless of the changes that are made, the major goals of the SIP [Schools Improvement Program] in each school will always be to have a positive effect on children's learning and to strengthen the educational program of the school (Santa Fe School District 1988, 2; cited in Carnoy and Macdonell 1990, 55).

The empowerment of teachers within the overall design of the Schools Improvement Program is based upon an apparent shift in decision-making power from the district office and state legislature to school committees comprised of teachers and school principals. These committees have been given control over curriculum and instruction, as well as the power to select principals. In one school, the committee decided not to replace a retiring principal and the teachers administer the school by committee (Carnoy and Macdonell 1990). This constitutes a significant degree of democratization.

However, given the history of control of educational policy by the state legislature in New Mexico and the retention of actual decision-making power by the district school board, the capacity of this school-based management plan to empower teachers may be severely limited. If school reform requires approval by the school board, do school committees possess full decision-making power? In this case, school committee autonomy is confined to the limits set by the board. In practice, this confinement could undermine teacher empowerment, especially if significant change in curriculum and instruction is sought. This retention of power may be designed to provide increased efficiency and implementation success without giving up managerial control. Given that the professionalization approach is based in part upon recent organizational reforms in business and industry, it is likely this is the orientation. Analysts argue that we have entered a new era of business management (e.g., Peters and Waterman 1984;

Reich 1983, 1991), a shift from hierarchical, bureaucratic systems of authority to more participatory, decentralized management structures. As Reich put it:

> In the era of human capital, an era that all industrialized nations are entering, high-volume, standardized production will to a great extent be replaced by flexible-system production, in which integrated teams of workers identify and solve problems. This new organization of work necessarily will be more collaborative, participatory, and egalitarian than is high-volume, standardized production, for the simple reason that initiative, responsibility, and discretion must be so much more widely exercised within it. Since its success depends on quickly indentifying and responding to opportunities in its rapidly changing environment, the flexible-system enterprise cannot afford rigidly hierarchical chains of authority (1983, 246).

Participatory decision making is conceived here as a means to efficient performance, rather then in terms of empowerment. The focus is on production rather than political equality. This position is premised on the proposition that when individuals are party to the policymaking process they gain "ownership" of those policies and in turn more effectively carry them out (David 1989). When ownership is achieved, innovations have a better chance of actually being implemented. In other words, partial participation is used to instill ownership in policy in order to increase implementation success without giving up managerial control—that is, to increase the efficiency of the system, not to empower its members. This is a view of decentralization as efficient. As Dachler and Wilpert suggest, decentralization premised on efficiency has a tendency to limit "participatory arrangements in scope and intensity, restricting them to issues surrounding task accomplishment, and characteristically leaves them under the complete control of management, so that there is no intended challenge to the basic power prerogatives of. . . leaders" (1978, 9). From this perspective, the professionalization approach to school-based management may be a continuation of the efficiency-scientific management tradition in school administration rather than a democratic revolution.

The retention of school board power, however, may be an attempt to serve wider community interests. In this case, a compound structure would exist; however, a means of school representation on the local board and the state legislature is lacking, thereby undermining the democratic legitimacy of the compound structure. This issue highlights the importance of intergovernmental relations in the context of school restructuring, a fundamental problem with both the professionalization and the empowerment approach to school-based management. To advocate decentralization without addressing intergovernmental relations is to marginalize the effect of school restructuring.

The Santa Fe plan exemplifies another central problem with the strictly professionalization approach to school restructuring in that it limits school-site decision making to professional educators, excluding parents, students, and citizens. From a developmental perspective, this limitation is problematic for it retains the philosophical position of Platonic guardianship in the sense that, although extended to teachers, a legitimate claim to decision making power is still based upon expertise. Expertise cannot be legitimately used as the overriding criteria for deciding broad policy issues that affect one's children or the future of the community (See chapter 3).

The Community Empowerment Approach to
School-Based Management

The community empowerment approach to school restructuring attempts to shift decision-making power to the client and the community. On the surface this approach is more democratic in that it offers greater opportunites for a larger number of interested parties to participate in school governance. However, it will be argued that the so-called community empowerment models of school-based management are also designed primarily to increase efficiency rather than to empower the community. Three prominent community empowerment models of school-based management are Dade County, Florida; Kentucky; and Chicago[5]

In July 1986, the Dade County (Miami) school district, the fourth-largest school district in the United States, adopted a school-based management-shared decision-making pilot program. The program was written into the teachers' collective bargaining agreement, evolving out of the earlier implementation of faculty councils in individual schools. Thirty-two schools were selected to participate in the program. The decision making structure is centered on school councils, which have taken various names such as governing council, education cabinet, and decision-making committee. The school councils are comprised of between five to twelve members, including the principal, union steward, an elected teacher, and student, staff, and parent representatives. These councils serve as the central decision-making body for each school in addition to a number of subcommittees concerning curriculum, student management, scheduling, and school-community relations that are comprised of different interest groups, parents, students, and teachers. The subcommittees examine issues and then make recommendations, submitting an agenda to the central school council for final deliberation and decision. Decisions are normally taken by majority vote (Cistone, Fernandez, and Tornillo 1989; Hanson 1990).

Evolving out of faculty councils and being based upon the collective bargaining agreement between the teachers and the school district, the Dade County model of school-based managment was originally based upon the professionalization approach, however, it has expanded its participatory scope to include clients. Nonclient citizens are not represented. As a whole, the Dade County example incorporates many of the features of a developmental model. It includes representation of a number of interest groups, excluding citizens; a wide array of decisional content open to deliberation; and a compound structure encompassing both direct and indirect participation, direct participation in agenda-setting and indirect participation in final deliberation and decision.

However, the degree of participation is significantly limited by the fact that principals retain veto power in the school councils. In effect, this veto provision delimits the degree of participation from full to partial, reducing the school councils and subcommittees to consultative bodies, again a method of accounting for the preferences of the community without truly empowering it. This orientation is inherent in the Kentucky school reform as well.

In June 1989, the Kentucky supreme court issued an opinion that held the state's entire public school system unconstitutional, primarily on the grounds that it was discriminatory and violated the constitutional right of all children to receive an adequate education.

This decision applies to the entire sweep of the system—all its parts and parcels. This decision applies to the statutes creating, implementing and financing the *system* and to all regulations, etc., pertaining thereto. This decision covers the creation of local school districts, school boards, and the Kentucky Department of Education to the Minimum Foundation Program and Power Equalization Program. It covers school construction and maintenance, teacher certification—the whole gamut of the common school system of Kentucky. . .Since we have, by this decision, declared the system of common schools in Kentucky to be unconstitutional, Section 183 [the section of the school code mandating a common school system] places an absolute duty on the General Assembly to re-create, restablish a new system of common schools in the Commonwealth. . . .We view this decision as an opportunity for the General Assembly to launch the Commonwealth into a new era of educational opportunity which will ensure a strong economic, cultural and political future. (*Rose v. Council for Better Education, Inc.*, Ky., No. 88-SC-804-TG Sept. 28, 1989, 66, 67–68).

The General Assembly responded, in July 1989, by appointing the Task Force on Education Reform, comprised of the house and senate leadership as well as representatives appointed by the governor. The Task Force's final report was enacted into law as the Education Reform Act of 1990 (House Bill 940 as enacted) on April 11, 1990 (Miller, Noland, and Schaaf 1990). The Education Reform Act constitutes a mandate and blueprint for the entire reformulation of the Kentucky public school system, affecting approximately 1,300 schools.

An important feature of this reform is the mandate for the adoption of school-based management by every school in the state by July 1996. Each school will have a council comprised of two parents, three teachers, and the principal; the parents and teachers will be elected. The councils are charged with the formulation of a broad array of policies concerning curriculum, assignment of staff time, assignment of students to classes, daily and weekly schedules, the use of school facilities, instruction, discipline, extracurricular programs, and operational funds alloted to the school (Miller et al. 1990; Van Meter 1991). Decisions are to be taken on the basis of consensus, and council meetings are to be open to the public, although the general public has no input in policy formation (Van Meter 1991). Approximately 150 schools have formed councils (Kentucky Department of Education 1991).

It is stipulated, however, that school policy is to be formulated within the framework of district and state policy. Although the powers of the school council seem to be extensive, this provision reduces the decision making power of the council. Although the reform act mandates school-based decision making, it reserves significant power at the state level. For example, there is an overarching concern in the reform act for accountability, embodied in the establishment of a Council on Performance charged with developing standards for assessing statewide student achievement. In fact, it is stipulated that those schools deemed "successful" in terms of student achievement be given monetary rewards from the state (sections 5, 6). In addition, an Office of Educational Accountability has been established to execute the state assessment system.

Although the role of the Kentucky Department of Education is perceived by Commissioner of Education Thomas Boysen as a service-oriented role to local districts wherein the state is to "stimulate without regulating and to challenge without oppressing. . . striving to de-emphasize the enforcement and compliance role of the department" (Boysen 1991, 16), the assessment provisions as well as the constitutional retention of power by the state without providing for genuine representation threatens to undermine the effacacy of school-based decision making. Those who formulate the standards on which evaluations are based will control the behavior of those who are evaluated. By controlling the standards of evaluation the state controls the curriculum and instructional method employed as well as the nature of extracurricular activities, thereby effectively undermining the decision-making power of the local school council. This is an attempt to increase efficiency without giving up control. A school-based governance system and state-formulated accountability measures are inherently contradictory. If the local school is not directly represented on the state level, community empowerment inherent in the school-based decision making system will be effectively undermined by the retention of state control. Although advocating school-based decision making, by placing significant power on the state level without genuine local representation the Kentucky Reform Act embodies the efficiency orientation to decentralization.

The Chicago plan for school reform (General Assembly of the State of Illinois 1989) moves the closest to genuine democratic empowerment but still falls short. The central feature of the Chicago plan is the establishment of local school councils. These councils consist of the principal and ten elected members: six parents, two community members, and two teachers. Each elected member is elected from within his or her respective groups. Thus, parents elect parents and teachers elect teachers. The local school council is responsible for evaluating the performance of the principal, who serves under a four-year performance contract. The council has the power to fire and replace a principal whose performance is substandard. The council is charged with approving the expenditure plan, based upon a lump-sum allocation, that the principal prepares. The council is also charged with making recommendations to the principal concerning textbook selections, advising the principal concerning attendance and disciplinary policies, and approving the school improvement plan, a plan mandated by the reform legislation for the improvement of every school in the city. It is stipulated that the local school council "shall convene at least 2 well-publicized meetings annually with its entire school community. These meetings shall include presentation of the proposed local school improvement plan, of the proposed school expenditure plan, and the annual report, and shall provide an opportunity for public comment" (General Assembly of the State of Illinois 1989, 1276).

In addition, subdistrict councils have been established and are comprised of one parent or community member from each school council within the subdistrict. These members are elected from within their respective school councils. The duties of this council are to promote coordination and communication among local school councils and school staffs; to disseminate research concerning innovative educational techniques; to promote and conduct training of local school councils; to promote and coordinate joint school operations; and to provide voluntary dispute resolution of problems encountered by local school councils. The subdistrict council is also charged with hiring and evaluating a subdistrict superintendent. This superintendent is responsible for monitoring the performance of individual schools and identifying failing schools.

The final level of the governance structure is the board of education. Which is to be appointed by the mayor from a list of candidates nominated by each local school council. The board is charged with exercising "general supervision and jurisdiction over the public education and the public school system of the city" (1989, 1282). It has the power to establish and maintain schools and educational facilities, to divide the city into subdistricts and apportion pupils to schools, to establish and approve citywide curriculum objectives and standards, to employ nonteaching personnel, to develop school facilities improvement and maintenance policy, among other powers.

As a whole, the Chicago plan comprises a compound structure with the separation of various powers and duties on different levels and representation based upon the local school. It constitutes a significant departure from the centralized system born in the Progressive Era. It returns significant control of local schools to local representatives. It provides increased opportunity for participation, at least in an indirect format, to teachers, parents, and citizens. Decision making is no longer insulated from the influence of these groups.

From the developmental perspective, however, the Chicago plan fails to provide an adequate degree of direct participation. The participation of the average teacher, parent, and citizen is limited to the selection of representatives. Although in a decentralized structure participation in the selection of representatives may involve initial agenda-setting and alternative specification, the provision for two annual meetings wherein only public comment is sought does not allow significant participation in long-range agenda-setting, alternative formation, or the selection process. In addition, the local school council is more of a ratifying than a legislative body in that its basic power is that of approval or disapproval. It is limited to approving the expenditure plan and school improvement plan submitted by the principal, and it is limited to advisement concerning textbook selection and attendance and disciplinary policy. Although it holds the power to replace the principal if unsatisfactory, the school council itself is not significantly involved in the formulation of policy. It merely ratifies policy already formulated. However, given the decentralized nature of the system, informal participation in policy formation may be widespread.

In addition, the Chicago plan uses a weighted representative system in reverse of Mill's system. School council representation is not weighted in favor of professional competence, but in favor of parents. This is an attempt to empower the clients of the school. However, in a 6–1 decision handed down on November 30, 1990, the Illinois supreme court ruled that this weighting violated the one-person, one-vote principle established by the U.S. Supreme Court, thereby making the school reform law that mandates the school-based management plan unconstitutional (Education Week, December 12, 1990). The lawsuit leading to this decision was brought by the Chicago Principals Association and other school officals whose power, in an authoritarian sense, has been undermined by the reform. The Court was willing to hold its mandate to give officials sufficient time to take legislative action in response to the ruling (Education Week, December 5, 1990).[6]

Although the Chicago plan takes important steps in the direction of a developmentally participative governance system, it falls short by not providing formal opportunities for nonrepresentatives—and for that matter representatives—to participate fully and directly in the policymaking process. In addition, the emphasis on community empowerment threatens to undermine the imperative of professionalization. What is needed is a balanced, integrated system of governance that provides full and equal participation for all parties.

Although the Chicago plan does move in a developmental direction in that it seems to be genuinely premised on empowerment rather than efficiency, provisions for more extensive full and direct participation are called for if the plan's developmental intentions are to be fulfilled.

Conclusion

The school-based management movement as represented by the four models discussed constitutes a significant departure from the bureaucratic, centralized elite democratic system of school governance born in the Progressive Era. It constitutes a significant movement toward a democratic system of school governance in that it increases the degree of participation by teachers, parents, citizens, and students in the educational policy process. However, it does not go far enough in terms of democratic empowerment. Its shortcomings center on two fundamental flaws.

First, there is a tendency to favor either professionalization or community empowerment, one at the expense of the other. When a plan favors professionalization, it tends to delimit the participation of parents, citizens, and students. When a plan favors community empowerment, it tends to undermine teacher professionalization. What is needed is a balanced, comprehensive system of governance that increases professionalization while simultaneously empowering the community. Although these two goals may seem contradictory, a system of governance that provides an equal degree of decision-making power to all parties and is based upon consensus can empower both groups through collective deliberation.

Second, the retention of administrative, district, and state control without genuine representation reduces school-based management to preference accounting in order to increase efficiency through the fostering of ownership, thereby undermining genuine democratic empowerment of local schools. From this perspective, school-based management maybe more of a continuation of the efficiency tradition in school administration rather than a democratic revolution. This conclusion highlights the importance of intergovernmental relations in the context of school restructuring. A more complete conception of participatory decision making would integrate efficiency with developmental and empowerment considerations. This integration would entail a genuinely representative compound structure. For school-based management to be significant in terms of a real shift in power, the school committee must share power with other governmental units in the context of overlapping jurisdictions. It cannot be subject to regulation without representation and be a site where real decision-making power is exercised.

As discussed in chapter 3 a compound structure with overlapping jurisdictions affording genuine representation cannot logically be achieved through a grant of authority, for in principle such a grant entails the retention of ultimate authority. Thus, for school-based management in the context of a federal system to constitute a real shift in power it must either entail delegation, deliberative opinion polling, and/or oversight juries. What is called for is the establishment of a genuine compound republic based upon direct participation and genuine representation.

The school-based management movement can be viewed as an attempt to move to a more representative system. However, the intergovernmental constraints discussed herein threaten to impede this achievement, in effect keeping school-based decision making on the fringe, giving an illusion of power through the allocation of partial participation in order to increase commitment and implementation success while preserving elite control. This provides a democratic veneer similar to the one used by the Educational Commission of the City of Chicago in 1898. From this perspective, although school-based management appears decentralized, it retains a significant, potentially debilitating, degree of elite control.

Epilogue

This book has been premised on the notion of constitutional choice, the possibility that we can, through reflective deliberation, choose our systems of institutional governance. The choice, however, is premised upon what we value. If we value efficiency over all, then bureaucracy and elite control will remain a prominent part of our institutional lives. However, in this book I have entertained an alternative. Bureaucracy and elite control are not inevitable. They have been chosen. Other possibilities exist. One is a system of governance premised upon the value of human development. If we value human development as the foundational ideal of formal schooling, then, it has been argued, the principles of participation, communication, association, nonviolence, and community should define our system of school governance. What would such a system of school governance look like? How would it operate? Within the theoretical parameters set by the principles of developmental democracy there are numerous possibilities. One combination of such possibilities has been entertained.

First, it has been argued that the basic structure of the decision-making system would entail an integrated, compound structure in the sense that the structure allows for direct participation in significant stages of the decision-making process while providing for the sharing of authority across levels of the structure. Second, within any compound structure there arises the question of representation. How can all participants be fully and genuinely represented on all levels of the structure? Delegation, deliberative opinion polling, and oversight juries taken separately or perhaps more fruitfully in combination seem to be viable forms of representation in terms of consistency with the principles of developmental democracy. Third, how will decisions be rendered? It has been argued that a strong democratic, creative consensus is more consistent with the principles of participation, communication, and nonviolence than majority rule, deference to expertise, a unified or a bargained consensus. However, it was also argued that although premised upon political equality, in order for the consensual process to constitute genuine equality in the face of social inequality certain features and safeguards must be

included: genuine dialogue, transformational leadership, political
education and organization, due process based upon nonrepression
and nondiscrimination, and juridical standards. Taken in combination
these design features would comprise a system of school governance
wherein policy would emerge from the bottom up, informed and crafted
by direct participation in a deliberative process. This process would
in turn provide an opportunity for the development of informed
educational participants.

A participatory system of school governance is not offered as a
panacea, however. This book has been premised upon the proposition
that a participatory system of school governance is a necessary but
not a sufficient condition for educational excellence. A number of other
conditions are necessary, perhaps the most important being financial
equality. Inequality in funding to provide education resources (books,
computers, libraries, counseling, and educationally conducive school
buildings and classrooms), smaller class sizes, and highly qualified
teachers, among other resources, undermines the possibility of an
excellent educational experience for every student. In fact, the gap
in educational expenditures between wealthy and poor school districts
is growing, exacerbated by a significant reduction of federal funding
(a drop of 33 percent in the 1980s) and a reduction in corporate
property tax payments to local governments (the corporate share of
local property taxes fell from 45 percent in 1957 to 16 percent in 1989)
among other causes (Kozol 1991; Reich 1991).

On the one hand, the democratic restructuring of individual
schools cannot compensate for gross financial inequities. Even if
impoverished schools are democratized, they will still lack the
necessary resources for educational renewal. On the other hand,
however, the democratization of the entire compound structure of
school governance, from local to state to federal, could provide a
genuine representation of the interests of all students, possibly leading
to a change in school finance in the direction of equal protection under
the law. As long as the privileged retain political control of school
finance, it is unlikely that equity will be achieved. Thus,
democratization, not of isolated schools but of the entire
intergovernmental system, constitutes the framework within which
equality and justice become possibilities.

The trend toward increasing centralization and inequality
signals a profound need for rethinking our systems of institutional
governance. If we are serious about democracy, and if we believe we
are capable of "establishing good government from reflection and
choice," then the formulation of proposals for the restructuring of

school governance in truly democratic directions is necessary step in the ongoing struggle for a democratic and just way of life.

Notes

Introduction

1. Implicit in the notion of constitutional choice is the idea that the choice of a particular governance system will be made through a process of democratic deliberation.

2. The use of the passive voice to describe constitutional choice disguises the fact that someone engages in this process. In fact, the question of "who decides" is precisely the substance of political theory. This question is especially important when considering different conceptions of democracy, for it is precisely the extent to which decision-making power is shared that determines the form of democracy (e.g., direct democracy versus republicanism). Who decides, however, is contingent upon what values are being pursued. The concept of constitutional choice is fundamentally conditional in that, given a particular value, certain principles and design specifications follow. The question of who decides is in the end contemplated and decided when considering design specificatons.

3. The exception is, of course school-based management approaches that move toward greater democratization. These approaches will be discussed in chapter 4.

4. The national debate over political structure in the Progressive Era constitutes one of the few clear instances of major deliberation concerning the nature of schooling in American educational history. This was especially true in the case of Chicago, where the Chicago Teachers Federation and its supporters articulated an alternative political philosophy to the one espoused by people whom Tyack (1974) refers to as "administrative progressives" and "corporate liberals," which formed the philosophical basis of their twenty-year campaign in opposition to centralization. As Murphy notes, the "CTF launched the strongest opposition to school centralization in the country" (1981, 43).

5. This is a very diverse group, but they share a common thread: they all argue for participatory democracy on the basis of human development. Their position will be given full treatment in chapter 2.

6. The validity of the realist theory of universals has been debated since Plato conceived it. It has two fundamental problems: one metaphysical, the

other epistemological. First, it is unclear how particulars are related to the universals, that is, how the form of the particular is conferred onto it by the universal. If the universals are transcendent, as Plato maintains, then the problem of their relation to particulars becomes impossible to solve in principle, for transcendence denotes separation and duality rather than relatedness. The universal must in principle be separate from particulars, for they must be free of their relative imperfection and status in order to be universal. If immanent, they will become a relative part of the particular and, consequently, will no longer be universal (Woozley 1967). Second, if the universals are transcendent, how can we know them? Plato argues that our souls have epistemic acess to the Forms in the after-death realm, as depicted, for example, in the Myth of Er in Book 10 of the *Republic* (1979, 614a–621d). At birth (after reincarnation), our memory of them is lost to our conscious awareness, but the knowledge of them remains, a priori, in the soul waiting to be recollected (see the Meno, Plato 1956). By turning reason in the proper direction through education, the Forms can be recollected. Even in this case, however, one does not have direct access to the Form while alive; one can only access the "memory" of the Form. Thus, the question arises of the epistemic validity of the universals. The transcendent nature of the universals negates the possibility of epistemic access, which undermines any attempt to know them. Therefore, the realist theory of universals has formidable metaphysical and epistemological problems.

7. Ideologies in this sense are not representations of false consciousness, but are paradigmatic schema that attempt to make sense of experience. This is not to suggest, however, that particular ideologies never come to be hegemonic in a Gramscian sense. An ideology can "'saturate' our very consciousness, so that the educational, economic, and social world we interact with, and the commonsense interpretation we put on it, becomes the world *tout court,* the only world" (Apple 1979, 5; see also Boggs 1984). Any attempt to break through ideological hegemony by presenting an alternative worldview must also be seen as ideological, however.

8. In this sense, this book can be viewed as an attempt to build upon the insights of Haley and Young, although their conception of developmental democracy is limited to professionalization.

Chapter 1. The Chicago Dabate

1. It is important to note that a reverse process was occurring in Atlanta during the Progressive Era. Educational authority was centralized in Atlanta from the inception of the school system (Peterson 1985). Before the progressive reforms, the school system was under the "direction of elite 'citywide' interests" embodied in a school board comprised of members of the business and professional elite (Peterson 1985, 128). The restructuring of school governance in Atlanta shifted authority from the traditional elite "into the hands of

somewhat less prestigious men, including lawyers and other middle-class professionals, small businessmen, and men with political ties to the local labor movement" (130). This reform increased political representation in the school system in contrast to what occurred in northern cities.

2. For example, Margaret Haley argued that the commission "was nothing but a mouthpiece for Harper" (Reid 1982, 35).

3. State intervention in order to regulate the market economy as well as other social institutions is the central defining feature of corporate liberalism, whereas classical liberalism was premised on the limitation of state intervention in private enterprise (Weinstein 1968).

4. Ninety-seven percent of the teaching force was female at the time the report was published.

5. Of course, this brings up the issue of whether the Progressive Era was in fact progressive. From the perspective of this historical argument, the reforms of the period were not progressive in a democratic sense. Other historians see it differently, however; for example, see Cremin (1961). There were of course progressive proposals (e.g. Dewey). However, conservative, elite forces prevailed.

6. This is what I will define in chapter 3 as partial, indirect participation, a way to account for preferences without relinquishing real power. This is the degree and format of participation that school-based management models tend to possess (chapter 4).

7. "An Act to Amend the Act to Establish and Maintain a System of Free Schools" was approved April 20, 1917.

8. Here Haley equates democracy with liberalism. Their equivalence is not logically necessary. In fact, many argue that they are contradictory (e.g., Macpherson 1966; Paringer 1990). *Liberal* in this sense refers to freedom from constraint (negative freedom), whereas *democracy* refers to self-governance (positive freedom). Haley is arguing that liberty and democracy entail both negative and positive liberty, a view held by the ancient Greek democrats and the developmental theorists surveyed in this book.

9. Young was the first female school superintendent of any large city. She was hired by Dunne, who was sympathetic to a decentralized system of school governance. See Murphy (1981) and Hogan (1985) for more detail regarding Dunne and his board of education. This may be another example of indeterminance.

10. Here Young is advocating partial participation, which is very similar to the commission's councils. This finding suggests a contradiction between Young's developmental principles and her design specifications. It is essential that the principles and the design specifications be consistent.

Chapter 2. The Developmental Conception of Democracy

1. The values, principles, and design specifications derived from the political thought of these theorists are summarized in the conclusion to this chapter.

2. As Jane Roland-Martin (1985) points out, however, the pedagogical methods Rousseau advocates in *Emile* are manipulative and gender-biased, thereby rendering them incapable of helping to form an independent and compassionate private will. Rousseau conceives citizenship as an exclusively male role, thereby profoundly restricting his democratic vision. Nevertheless, the arguments he makes for men may have relevance for women as citizens as well.

3. Consensual decision making is discussed in detail in chapter 3 as well as in the section of this chapter on Gandhi.

4. The size principle was an important consideration for Madison and Hamilton as well. The choice is either to decentralize or to move to a representative system. The size principle, and consequently this choice, are discussed at length at the end of this chapter.

5. The elite democratic theorists discussed herein also recognize the importance of public opinion, but their solution is to control it and manufacture consent. Mill opts for the alternative to control: development. Instead of manipulating the public, Mill wants to develop the public so that they will be able to engage in deliberation, allowing public choice to be based on their genuine, deliberated consent.

6. Recall that, at least in terms of their rhetoric, enlightened despotism was the vision of the administrative progressives.

7. Given Boris Yeltsin's centralizing tendency, it is unclear whether Russia and the other former Soviet republics will remain politically centralized (See Cohen 1992).

8. For a summary of these design specifications, see Held (1987).

9. Decision-rules consistent with the value of development are discussed at the end of this chapter as well as in chapter 3.

10. Neglecting decision-rules highlights the fact that decentralization is not a sufficient condition for developmental democracy. Juridical procedures consistent with development are also necessary.

11. This discussion was presented originally at the annual meeting of the Philosophy of Education Society and published in their proceedings (Snauwaert 1992).

12. This notion of "family resemblance" is derived from Wittgenstein (1953).

13. For a discussion of degrees of participation consistent with this conception, see Bernstein 1982; Conway 1984; Dachler and Wilpert 1978; Hebden and Shaw 1977; IDE 1976; Jansen and Kissler 1987; King and van de Vall 1978; and Pateman 1970.

14. However, there is a danger in justifying participation on efficiency grounds in that there is a tendency to view partial and indirect participation as sufficient to meet efficiency requirements (Dachler and Wilpert 1978). This is a potential problem with school-based managment, discussed in Chapter Five.

15. A significant research tradition in contemporary political science suggests little empirical support for the existence of common interests. Rather individuals pursue their narrow self-interests, and anything resembling a public interest is merely an aggregate of individual self-interest. This theoretical perspective has become known as public choice theory and is primarily based upon microeconomics, which views the individual as a maximizer of self-interest (Kelman 1988). The origins of this tradition can be traced to Downs (1957), Buchanan and Tullock (1962), and Olson (1965). Downs puts forth the "self-interest axiom," the view that politics is "directed primarily toward selfish ends" (1957, 27–28). Buchanan and Tullock argue that "the average individual acts on the basis of the same over-all value scale when he participates in market activity and in political activity" (1962, 20). Olson (1965) argues that political organization on the basis of collective goals was irrational in terms of self-interest. Given the costs of participation and the remote probability that the individual's participation would have an impact, it is rational for the individual to be inactive. Although there is ample empirical support for the proposition that individuals are motivated by self-interest, evidence exists that they are also motivated by a regard for the well-being others and their community (e.g., Kelman 1988; Oliner and Oliner 1988). For example, the poor were neither a majority nor an organized interest in the 1960s and 1970s, yet a massive welfare program was enacted by Congress. Health, safety, and environmental regulation was established in spite of the opposition of well-organized, self-interested corporations. A massive program concerning education and rehabilitation for individuals with handicaps was established in the 1970s. As Reich suggests, these initiatives were enacted largely due to the fact that "they were thought to be good for *society*" (1988, 4, emphasis in original). From a normative perspective, given the impending ecological disaster, we must move away from self-interest toward a concern for the larger public, global interest if we are to survive.

Chapter 3. Design

1. Of course, free market theorists argue that the community is served through the "invisible hand" of the market. There is also another significant

problem with free market choice, in that it ignores the impact of social inequality on freedom of choice. This problem will be discussed in chapter 4.

2. Fishkin (1992) discusses the Athenian jury on pages 87–91. For a review and discussion of Fishkin, from which my presentation of Fishkin is based, see Snauwaert (1992).

3. Social democratization has to start somewhere, most likely from populist, grass-roots sources (Arendt 1962), and thus, although imperfect, school governance is a potential site. Ideally, the democratization of school governance would proceed simultaneously with the democratization of other social institutions.

4. Benjamin Barber's use of the word juridical is fundamentally different than Lowi's conception. Whereas Barber's concept of juridical refers to a deference to judicial standards that provide a ground for decision making, Lowi's concept of juridical refers to the detailed specification of policy.

Chapter 4. School Restructuring

1. Although the rhetoric of *A Nation at Risk* includes the liberal development of students and democratic citizenship, it conceives the basic purpose of schooling as economic.

2. For a critical analysis of *A Nation at Risk* see Apple (1988) and Beyer (1985).

3. This centralization is so extensive that Lowi (1979) maintains that it constitutes a second republic.

4. Perhaps an example of transformational leadership.

5. The discussion of Santa Fe, Dade County, Florida; Kentucky; and Chicago is not intended to provide a comprehensive survey of school-based management models. Rather, this list is intended to provide a sample. Models more consistent with the principles of developmental democracy may be in existence.

6. At the time of writing, legislative action had yet to be taken.

References

Arblaster, A. 1987. *Democracy*. Minneapolis: University of Minnesota Press.

Apple, M. W. 1979. *Ideology and curriculum*. Boston: Routledge & Kegan Paul.

———. 1982. *Education and power*. Boston: Routledge & Kegan Paul.

———. 1988. What reform talk does: Creating new inequalities in education. *Educational Administration Quarterly* 24:272–281.

Arendt, H. 1962. *On revolution*. New York: Penguin.

Bacharach, S. B., S. C. Bauer, and J. B. Shedd. 1986. The work environment and school reform. *Teachers College Record* 88:241–256.

Barber, B. R. 1984. *Strong democracy: Participatory politics for a new age*. Berkeley: University of California Press.

———. 1989. Public talk and civic action: Education for participation in a strong democracy. *Social Education* Oct:355–370.

Barrett, J. 1983. Immigrant workers in early mass production industry: Work rationalization and job control conflicts in Chicago's Packinghouses, 1900–1904. In *German workers in industrial Chicago, 1850–1910*, ed. H. A. Keil and J. B. Jentz, 104–24. DeKalb: Northern Illinois University Press.

Becker, C. L. 1958. *The declaration of independence: A study in in the history of political ideas*. New York: Vintage.

Becker, H. J., and J. Epstein. 1982. Parent involvement: A survey of teacher practices. *The Elementary School Journal* 83:85–102.

Beer, S. H. 1978. Federalism, nationalism, and democracy in America. *The American Political Science Review* 72:9–21.

Bendix, R. 1963. *Work and authority in industry*. New York: Harper Torch.

Benn, S. I. 1967. Democracy. In *The encyclopedia of philosophy*, ed. P. Edwards, 338–41. New York: Macmillan.

Bennis, W. G. 1984. Transformative power and leadership. In *Leadership and organizational culture*, ed. T. J. Sergiovanni and J. E. Corbally, 64–71. Urbana: University of Illinois Press.

Benson, N., and P. Malone. 1987. Teachers' beliefs about shared decision making and work alienation. *Education* 107:244–51.

Bentham, J. 1931. *The theory of legislation.* New York: Ogden.

Berger, P., and T. Luckman. 1966. *The social construction of reality.* Garden City, NY: Doubleday & Co.

Berlin, I. 1969. *Four essays on liberty.* Oxford: Oxford University Press.

Bernstein, P. 1982. Necessary elements for effective worker participation in decision-making. In *Workplace democracy and social change,* ed. F. Lindenfeld, and J. Rothschild-Whitt, 51–81. Boston: Porter Sargent.

Berry, W. 1987. *Home economics.* San Francisco: North Point Press.

Beyer, L. E. 1985. Educational reform: The political roots of national risk. *Curriculum Inquiry* 15:337–55.

Bhardwaj, R. K. 1980. *Democracy in India.* New Delhi: National Publishing House.

Boggs, C. 1984. *The two revolutions: Gramsci and the dilemmas of western Marxism.* Boston: South End Press.

Bolin, F. S. 1986. Empowering leadership. *Teachers College Record* 91:81–96.

Boulding, E. 1988. Building a global civic culture: Education for an interdependent world. New York: Teachers College Press.

Bowles, S., and H. Gintis. 1976. *Schooling in capitalist America.* New York: Basic Books.

_____. 1986. *Democracy and capitalism: Property, community, and the contradictions of social thought.* New York: Basic Books.

Boysen, T. C. 1991. Boysen to guide historic reform. *Ed News* [Kentucky Department of Education] 31:1–16.

Braverman, H. 1974. *Labor and monopoly capital: The degradation of work in the twentieth century.* New York: Monthly Review Press.

Bridges, E. M. 1967. A model for shared decision making in the school principalship. *Educational Administration Quarterly* 3:49–61.

Buchanan, J., and G. Tullock. 1962. *The calculus of consent.* Ann Arbor: University of Michigan Press.

Burawoy, M. 1978. Toward a Marxist theory of the labor process: Braverman and beyond. *Politics and Society* 8:247–312.

Burns, J. M. 1978. *Leadership*. New York: Harper and Row.

Callahan, R. 1962. *Education and the cult of efficiency: A study of social forces that have shaped the administration of public schools*. Chicago: University of Chicago Press.

Carnegie Commission on Teaching as a Profession. 1986. *A Nation prepared: Teachers for the 21st century*. Hyattsville, MD: Author.

Carnoy, M., and J. MacDonell. 1990. School district restructing in Santa Fe, New Mexico. *Educational Policy* 4:49–64.

Cattermole, J., and N. Robinson. 1985. Effective home/school/communications: From the parents' perspective. *Phi Delta Kappan* 67:48–50.

Chandler, A. D. 1977. *The visible hand: The managerial revolution in American business*. Cambridge: Harvard University Press.

Chatterjee, D. K. 1984. *Gandhi and constitution making in India*. New Delhi: Associated Publishing House.

Chicago Board of Education (1899). *55 annual report of the board of education, 1898–1899*. Chicago: Author.

Chubb, J. E., and T. M. Moe. 1990. *Politics, markets, and America's schools*. Washington, DC: The Brookings Institution.

Cistone, P. J. 1989. School-based management/shared decision making: Perestroika in educational governance. *Education and Urban Society* 21:363–65.

Cistone, P. J., J. A. Fernandez, and P. L. Tornillo. 1989. School-based management/shared decision making in Dade county (Miami). *Education and Urban Society* 21:393–402.

Cohen, S. F. 1992. What's really happening in Russia. *The Nation* 254:259–68.

Commission on Excellence in Education 1983. *A nation at risk*. Washington, DC: Author.

Conley, S. C. 1989. "Who's on first?" School reform, teacher participation, and the decision-making process. *Education and Urban Society* 21: 366–79.

Conway, J. 1984. Myth, mystery, and mastery of participative decision-making in education. *Educational Administration Quarterly* 50:11–40.

Cookson, P. W. 1991. Politics, markets, and America's schools: A review. *Teachers College Record* 93:156–60.

Coombs, F. S. 1987. The effects of increased state control on local school district governance. Paper presented at the annual meeting of the American Educational Research Association, Washington, DC, April 20–24.

Coons, J. E. and Sugarman, S. D. 1978. *Education by choice: The case for family control.* Berkeley: University of California Press.

Cremin, L. 1961. *The transformation of the school: Progressivism in American education, 1876–1957.* New York: Random House.

Cronin, J. M. 1973. *The control of urban schools: Perspective on the power of educational reformers.* New York: The Free Press.

Cropsey, J. 1989. Karl Marx. In *History of political philosophy,* ed. L. Straus and J. Cropsey. Chicago: The University of Chicago Press.

Crozier, M., S. P. Huntington, and J. Watannki. 1975. *The crisis of democracy.* New York: New York University Press.

Dachler, P. H., and B. Wilpert. 1978. Conceptual dimensions and boundaries of participation in organizations: A critical evaluation. *Administrative Science Quarterly* 23:1–39.

Dahl, R. A. 1956. *A preface to democratic theory.* Chicago: University of Chicago Press.

_____. 1967. *Pluralist democracy in the United States: Conflict and consent.* Chicago: Rand McNally.

_____. 1971. *After the revolution: Authority in a good society.* New Haven: Yale University Press.

_____. 1985. *A preface to economic democracy.* Berkeley: University of California Press.

David, J. L. 1989. Synthesis of research on school-based managment. *Educational Leadership* 46:45–52.

Dewey, J. 1910. *The influence of Darwin on philosophy.* New York: Henry Holt and Company.

_____. 1916. *Democracy and education.* New York: Free Press.

_____. 1927. *The public and its problems.* Chicago: Swallow Press.

_____. 1937. Education and social change. *Social Frontier* 3:235–237.

_____. 1946. Democracy and educational administration. In *Problems of men.* New York: Philosophical Library.

_____. 1948. *Reconstruction in philosophy.* Boston: Beacon Press.

_____. 1988. *Liberalism and social action*, In J. Gouinlock, *Excellence in public discourse.* New York: Teachers College Press.

Dilger, R. J. (ed.). 1986. *American intergovernmental relations today: Perspectives and controversies.* Englewood Cliffs, NJ: Prentice-Hall.

Downs, A. 1957. *An economic theory of democracy.* New York: Harper and Brothers.

Edwards, R. 1979. *Contested terrain: The transformation of the workplace in the twentieth century.* New York: Basic Books.

Educational Commission of the City of Chicago 1898. *The report of the educational commission of the city of Chicago.* Chicago: Author.

Eliot, C. 1989. The function of education in a democracy. In *Foundations of educational policy in the United States,* ed. J. Bennett et al., 193–96. Needham Heights, MA: Ginn Press.

Elmore, R. F. 1978. Organizational models of social program implementation. *Public Policy* 26:185–228.

_____. 1987. Reform and the culture of authority in schools. *Educational Administration Quarterly* 23:60–78.

_____. 1988. Models of restructuring schools. Paper presented at the annual meeting of the American Educational Research Association, New Orleans.

Epstein, J. L. 1986. Parents' reactions to teacher practices of parent involvement. *The Elementary School Journal* 86:277–294.

_____. 1987. Effects of teacher practices of parent involvement on student achievement in reading and math. In *Literacy through family, community, and school interaction, ed. S. Silver, 1#24. Greenwich, CT: JAI Press.*

Erlandson, D. A., and S. L. Bifano. 1987. Teacher empowerment: What research says to the principal. *NASSP Bulletin* 71:31–35.

Farrar, C. 1988. *The origins of democratic thinking: The invention of politics in classical Athens.* New York: Cambridge University Press.

Fischer, L. 1963. *The essential Gandhi.* London: Allen and Unwin.

Fisher, R., and W. Ury. 1983. *Getting to yes.* New York: Penguin.

Fishkin, J. S. 1991. *Democracy and deliberation: New directions for democratic reform.* New Haven: Yale University Press.

Foster, W. 1986. *Paradigms and promises: New approaches to educational administration.* Buffalo, NY: Prometheus Books.

Freire, P. 1970. *The pedagogy of the oppressed.* New York: Seabury Press.

Friedman, M. 1962. *Capitalism and freedom.* Chicago: University of Chicago Press.

Friedman, M., and R. Friedman. 1979. *Free to choose: A personal statement.* New York: Harcourt Brace Jovanovich.

Gandhi, M. K. 1962. *Village swaraj.* Ahmedabad: Navajivan Publishing House.

_____. 1966. *The village reconstruction.* Bombay: Bharatiya Vidya Bhavan.

Geisert, G. 1988. Participatory management: Panacea or hoax? *Educational Leadership* 46:59–69.

General Assembly of the State of Illinois. 1989. Schools and school districts: Chicago school reform, *Public Act 86–124.* Springfield: Author.

Goodlad, J. 1984. *A place called school: Prospects for the future.* New York: MacGraw Hill.

Grady, R. C. 1984. Juridical democracy and democratic values: An evaluation of Lowi's alternative to interest group liberalism. *Polity* 16:404–22.

Grant, G. 1985. The character of education and the education of character. *Kettering Review* Fall:51–52.

Gross, R. and Gross, B. (ed.). 1985. *The great school debate.* New York: Touchstone.

Guthrie, J. W. 1980. An assessment of educational policy research. *Educational Evaluation and Policy Analysis* 2:41–55.

_____. 1986. School-based managment: The next needed educational reform. *Phi Delta Kappan* 68:305–09.

Gutman, A. 1987. *Democratic education.* Princeton: Princeton University Press.

Haber, S. 1964. *Efficiency and uplift: Scientific management in the progressive era, 1890–1920.* Chicago: University of Chicago Press.

Haley M. A. 1903a. Comments on the new education bill. *CTF Bulletin,* January 23. Chicago Historical Society.

_____. 1903b. *CTF bulletin,* March 6. Chicago Historical Society.

_____. 1904. Why teachers should organize. *Addresses and proceedings of the national education organization,* 145–52. Chicago Historical Society.

_____. 1915. *Margaret A. Haley's bulletin*. Chicago: Chicago Historical Society.

Hanson, E. M. 1990. School-based management and educational reform in the United States and Spain. *Comparative Education Review* 34:523–37.

Hays, S. P. 1964. The politics of refrom in municipal government in the progressive era. *Pacific Northwest Quarterly*, October, 157–69.

_____. 1980. *American political history as social analysis*. Knoxville: University of Tennessee Press, 244–63.

Hebden, J. E., and G. H. Shaw. 1977. *Pathways to participation*. London: Associated Press.

Held, D. 1987. *Models of democracy*. Palo Alto, CA: Stanford University Press.

Heller, A. 1991. The concept of the political. In *Political theory today*, ed. D. Held. Stanford, CA: Standford University Press.

Herman, E. 1992. Democratic media. *Z Papers* 1:23–30.

Herman, E., and N. Chomsky. 1988. *Manufacturing consent: The political economy of the mass media*. New York: Pantheon Books.

Hess, G. A. 1991. *School restructuring, Chicago style*. Newbury Park, CA: Corwin Press.

Hirst, P. H. 1973. Liberal education and the nature of knowledge. In *The philosopy of education*, ed. R. S. Peters, 87–111. Oxford: Oxford University Press.

Hobsbawm, E. J. 1987. *The age of empire, 1875–1914*. New York: Pantheon Books.

Hogan, D. J. 1985. *Class and reform: School and society in Chicago, 1880–1930*. Philadelphia: University of Pennsylvania Press.

Holmes Group. 1986. *Tomorrow's teachers: A report of the Holmes Group*. Lansing, MI: Author.

Howe, H. 1991. Thoughts on choice. *Teachers College Record* 93:168–73.

IDE [International Research Group]. 1976. Industrial democracy in Europe: An international comparative study. *Social Science Information* 15:177–203.

Iyer, R. 1983. *The moral and political thought of Mahatma Gandhi*. 2d ed. New York: Concord Grove Press.

_____. 1986. *The moral and political writings of Mahatma Gandhi: Civilization, politics and religion.* Oxford: Clarendon Press.

Jaeger, W. 1953. *The Greeks and the education of man.* Annandale-on-Hudson, NY: Bard College Papers.

_____. 1965. *Paideia: The ideals of Greek culture*, v.1, New York: Oxford University Press.

Jansen, P., and L. Kissler. 1987. Organization of work by participation? A French–German comparison. *Economic and Industrial Democracy* 8:379–409.

Johnston, G. S., and V. Germinario. 1985. Relationship between teacher decisional status and loyalty. *The Journal of Educational Administration* 23:91–105.

Keller, G. 1987. *Academic strategy: The management revolution in American higher education.* Baltimore: John Hopkins University Press.

Kelman, S. 1988. Why public ideas matter. In *The power of public ideas*, ed. R. B. Reich. Cambridge, MA: Ballinger Publishing.

Kentucky Department of Education 1991. *Executive summary of KERA 1990 implementation.* Lexington: Author.

King, C. D., and M. van de Vall. 1978. *Models of industrial democracy: Consultation, co-determination and worker's management.* New York: Mouton Publishing.

Kingdon, J. W. 1984. *Agendas, alternatives, and public policies.* Boston: Little, Brown and Company.

Kolko, G. 1963. *The triumph of conservatism: A reinterpretation of American history, 1900–1916.* Glencoe, IL: Free Press.

Kozol, J. 1991. *Savage inequalities: Children in America's schools.* New York: Crown Publishers.

Kuhn, T. S. (1970). *The structure of scientific revolutions.* Chicago: University of Chicago Press.

Lindquist, K. M., and J. J. Mauriel. 1989. School-based management: Doomed to failure? *Education and Urban Society* 21:403–16.

Lipsky, M. 1980. *Street-level bureaucracy.* New York: Russell Sage.

Locke, J. 1947. *Second treatise on civil government.* New York: Random House.

Locke, E. A., and D. M. Schweiger. 1979. Participation in decision-making: One more look. In *Research in organizational behavior*, ed. B. M. Staw, 1–32. Greenwich, CT: JAI Press.

Lomotey, K., and A. D. Swanson. 1989. Urban and rural schools research: Implications for school governance. *Education and Urban Society* 21:436–54.

Lortie, D. C. 1975. *Schoolteacher: A sociological study*. Chicago: University of Chicago Press.

Lowi, T. J. 1979. *The end of liberalism: The second republic of the United States*. New York: Norton.

Macpherson, C. B. 1966. *The real world of democracy*. New York: Oxford University Press.

_____. 1973. *Democratic theory: Essays in retrieval*. New York: Oxford University Press.

_____. 1977. *The life and times of liberal democracy*. London: Oxford University Press.

_____. 1981. Pluralism, individualsim, and participation. *Economic and Industrial Democracy* 1:21–30.

Magdid, H. M. 1989. John Stuart Mill. In *History of political philosophy*, ed. L. Strauss and J. Cropsey. Chicago: The University of Chicago Press.

Majone, G., and A. Wildavsky. 1984. Implementation as evolution. In *Implementation*, ed. J. Pressman and A. Wildavsky, 163–80. Berkeley: University of California Press.

Mannheim, K. 1957. *Systematic sociology*. New York: Grove Press.

_____. 1960. *Ideology and utopia*. London: Routledge & Kegan Paul.

Marx, K. 1983. *The portable Karl Marx*, ed. E. Kamenka. New York: Penguin Books.

Mill, J. S. 1861. *Considerations on representative government*. London: Parker, Son, and Bourn.

_____. 1947. *On Liberty*. New York: Random House.

Miller, H. M., K. Noland, and J. Schaff. 1990. *A guide to the Kentucky reform act of 1990*. Frankfurt: Legislative Research Commission.

Mintzberg, H. 1987. Crafting strategy. *Harvard Business Review* July:66–75.

Miskel, C., and E. Gerhardt. 1974. Perceived bureaucracy, teacher conflict, cental life interests, voluntraism, and job satisfaction. *Journal of Educational Administration* 12:84–97.

Mohrman, A. M., R. A. Cooke, and S. A. Mohrman. 1978. Participation in decision making: A multidimensional perspective. *Educational Administration Quarterly* 14:13–29.

Montgomery, D. 1979. *Workers' control in America: Studies in the history of work, technology, and labor struggles.* New York: Cambridge University Press, ch.5.

Murphy, J. T. 1989. The paradox of decentralizing schools: Lessons from business, government, and the Catholic church. *Phi Delta Kappan* 70:808–12.

Murphy, M. 1981. From artisan to semi-professional: White collar unionism among Chicago public school teachers, 1870–1930. Doctoral dissertation, University of California, Davis.

National Governors' Association. 1986. *Time for results: The governors' 1991 report on education.* Washington, DC: Center for Policy Research and Analysis.

Nelson, D. 1975. *Managers and workers: Origins of the new factory system in the United States, 1880–1920.* Madison: University of Wisconson Press.

Nicholson, L. J. 1986. *Gender and history.* New York: Columbia University Press.

Okin, S. M. 1991. Gender, the public and the private. In *Political theory today,* ed. D. Held. Stanford, CA: Stanford University Press.

Oliner, S. P., and P. M. Oliner. 1988. *The altruistic personality: Rescuers of Jews in Nazi Europe.* New York: Free Press.

Olson, M. 1965. *The logic of collective action.* Cambridge, MA: Harvard University Press.

Ostrom, V. 1985. The meaning of federalism in the *Federalist*: A critical examination of the Diamond thesis. *Publius: The Journal of Federalism* 15:1–22.

————. 1987. *The political theory of a compound republic: Designing the American experiment.* 2d. ed. Lincoln: University of Nebraska Press.

Pagano, J. A. 1991. *Exiles and communities: Teaching in the patriarchal wilderness.* Albany: SUNY Press.

Paringer, W. A. 1990. *John Dewey and the paradox of liberal reform.* Albany: SUNY Press.

Pateman, C. 1970. *Participation and democratic theory*. London: Cambridge University Press.

_____. 1975. A contribution to the political theory of organizational democracy. In *Organization democracy: Participation and self-management*, ed. G. D. Garson and M. P. Smith. Beverly Hills: Sage.

_____. 1980. Women and consent. *Political Theory* 8:149–68.

_____. 1983a. Feminist critiques of the public/private dichotomy. In *Public and private in social life*, ed. S. I. Benn and G. F. Caus. London: Croom Helm.

_____. 1983b. Feminism and democracy. In *Democratic theory and practice*, ed. G. Duncan. Cambridge: Cambridge University Press.

_____. 1984. The shame of the marriage contract. In *Women's views of the political world of men*, ed. J. Stiehm. New York: Transnational Publishers.

_____. 1985. *The problem of political obligation: A critique of liberal theory*. Berkeley: University of California Press.

Peterson, P. 1985. *The politics of school reform, 1870–1940*. Chicago: University of Chicago Press, ch. 6.

Peters, B. G. 1984. *The politics of bureaucracy*. 2d ed. New York: Longmans.

Peters, T. J. , and R. H. Waterman, Jr. 1984. *In search of excellence: Lessons from America's best-run companies*. New York: Harper and Row.

Pierce, L. C. 1980. *School-based management*. Eugene: Oregon School Study Council.

Plato 1956. Meno. In *Protagoras and Meno*, trans. W. K. C. Guthrie. New York: Penguin Books.

_____. 1979. *The Republic*, trans. R. Larson. Arlington Heights, IL: Harlan Davidson.

Reagan, R. 1986. 1982 state of the Union address. In *American intergovernmental relations today: Perspectives and controversies*, ed. R. L. Dilger. Englewood Cliffs, NJ: Prentice-Hall.

Reardon, B. A. 1988. *Comprehensive peace education: Educating for global responsibility*. New York: Teachers College Press.

Reich, R. B. 1983. *The next American frontier*. New York: Penguin.

_____. 1988. *The power of public ideas*. Cambridge, MA: Ballinger Publishing.

_____. 1991. *The work of nations*. New York: Vintage Books.

Reid, R. L., ed. 1982. *Battleground: The autobiography of Margaret A. Haley.* Urbana: University of Illinois Press.

Rein, M. 1976. *Social science and public policy.* New York: Penguin.

Rich, D. K. 1985. *The forgotten factor in school success: The family.* Washington, DC: Home and School Institute.

Rodriguez, A. et al. 1989. *Foundations of educational policy in the United States.* Needham Heights, MA: Ginn Press.

Roland-Martin, J. 1985. *Reclaiming a conversation.* New Haven: Yale University Press.

Rousseau, J. J. 1973. *The social contract and discourses,* trans. G. D. H. Cole. New York: Dutton, Everyman's Library.

————. 1979. *Emile; or on education,* trans. A. Bloom. New York: Basic Books.

Rutherford, W. L. 1985. School principals as effective leaders. *Phi Delta Kappan* 67:31–34.

Sabel, C. and J. Zeitlin. 1985. Historical alternatives to mass production. *Past and Present,* 108, 133–76.

Santa Fe School District 1988. *Rebuilding for the future.* Santa Fe, NM: Author.

Schumpeter, J. 1942. *Capitalism, socialism, and democracy.* London: Allen and Unwin.

Sharma, M. L. 1987. *Gandhi and democratic decentralization in India.* New Delhi: Deep and Deep Publications.

Sirianni, C. 1982. *Worker's control and socialist democracy: The soviet experience.* London: Verso Editions.

Sirotnik, K. A., and R. W. Clark. 1988. School-centered decision making and renewal. *Phi Delta Kappan 69:660–664.*

Snauwaert, D. T. 1992. Dewey's developmental conception of democracy: Implications for school governance. In *Philosophy of education 1991,* ed. M. Buchmann and R. E. Floden. Normal, IL: Philosophy of Education Society.

————. 1992. Reclaiming the lost treasure: Deliberation and strong democratic education. *Educational Theory* 42: 351-67.

Sprinthall, R. C., and N. A. Sprinthall. 1981. *Educational psychology: A developmental approach.* London: Addison Wesley Publishing.

Spring, J. 1988. *Conflict of interests: The politics of American education.* New York: Longman.

State of Illinois 1907. *Blue book of the state of Illinois.* Springfield: Author.

Stone, I. F. 1988. *The trial of Socrates.* Boston: Little, Brown.

Swanson, A. D. 1989. Restructuring educational governance: A challenge of the 1990s. *Educational Administration Quarterly* 25:268–93.

Tozer, S. E. 1987. Elite power and democratic ideals. In *Society as educator in an age of transition,* ed. K. D. Benne and S. E. Tozer, 186–225. Chicago: University of Chicago Press.

Tyack, D. B. 1967. *Turning points in American educational thought.* New York: John Wily and Sons.

———. 1974. *The one best system: A history of american urban education.* Cambridge: Harvard University Press.

Tyack, D. B. and E. Hansot, 1982. *Managers of virtue: Public school leadership in America, 1820–1980.* New York: Basic Books.

USDE 1984. *A nation responds.* Washington, DC: Author.

Van Meter, E. J. 1991. The Kentucky mandate: School-based decision making. *NASSP Bulletin* 75:52–62.

Walberg, H. J. 1984. Families as partners in educational productivity. *Phi Delta Kappan* 65:397–400.

Walberg, H. J., M. J. Bakalis, J. L. Bast, and S. Baer, 1988. *We can rescue our childern: the cure for Chicago's public school crisis—with lessons for the rest of America.* Chicago: URF Education Foundation.

———. 1989. Reconstructing the nation's worst schools. *Phi Delta Kappan* 70:802–05.

Weber, M. 1946. *Economy and society.* Berkeley: University of California Press.

Weick, K. E. 1976. Educational organizations as loosely coupled systems. *Administrative Science Quarterly* 21:1–19.

Weinstein, J. 1968. *The corporate ideal in the liberal state: 1900–1918.* Boston: Beacon Press.

Wells, A. S. 1991. Choice in education: Examining the evidence on equity. *Teachers College Record* 93:138–55.

Wirt, F. 1977. School policy culture and state decentraliztion. In *The politics of education,* ed. J. D. Scribner. Chicago: University of Chicago Press.

Wittgenstein, L. 1953. *Philosophical investigations.* New York: Macmillan.

Woozley, A. D. 1967. Universals. In *The encyclopedia of philosophy*, ed. P. Edwards, 194–206. New York: Macmillan.

Yarbrough, J. 1985. Rethinking the *Federalist*'s view of federalism. *Publius: The Journal of Federalism* 15:31–53.

Yates, D. A. 1977. *The ungovernable city*. Cambridge, MA: MIT Press.

Young, E. F. 1901. *Isolation in the school*. Chicago: University of Chicago Press.

Zeitlin, I. M. 1987. *Ideology and the development of sociological theory*, 3d ed. Englewood Cliffs, NJ: Prentice-Hall.

Index

WITHDRAWN